BEYOND THE RED LETTERS

BY **RON KECK**

and Brian Daniel

MARK: Beyond the Red Letters

Published by Serendipity House Publishers
Nashville, Tennessee

ISBN: 978-1-5749-4341-2
Item No.: 005038468

Dewey Decimal Classification: 226.3
Subject Headings: BIBLE. N.T. MARK--STUDY

To purchase additional copies of this resource or other studies:
ORDER ONLINE at www.SerendipityHouse.com;
WRITE Serendipity House, One LifeWay Plaza, Nashville, TN 37234-0175
FAX (615) 277-8181 ~ PHONE (800) 525-9563

1-800-525-9563
www.SerendipityHouse.com

Printed in the United States of America
14 13 12 11 10 09 08 1 2 3 4 5 6 7 8 9 10

MARK
BEYOND THE RED LETTERS

CONTENTS

Other great Serendipity Larger Story resources ...

MORE.

More depth, more meaning, more life.

Something inside us yearns for more from life, God, and Bible study than we've experienced. Discovering truth through Bible study is more than breaking a verse down to its smallest parts and deconstructing a passage word-by-word. There is context and experience, mystery and stor that all go into fully understanding the living Word of God. The essence of the whole is more than the sum of its parts. Serendipity acknowledges that story is the language of the heart, anc without it, we can miss the wonder and power of the message. MORE looks at the Bible and life within the context of the Larger Story—the eternity that God has written on our hearts. Dare tc discover and experience more of life, more of God, and more of your role in the Grand Adventur

***Song of Songs: The Epic Romance* | 1574943405**
***Mark: Beyond the Red Letters* | 1574943413**
***Job: A Messy Faith* | 1574943464**
***Colossians: Embrace the Mystery* | 1574944150**

GOD AND THE ARTS

Where faith intersects life.

Stories, great and small, share the same essential structure because every story we tell borrows its power from a Larger Story. What we sense stirring within is a heart that is made for a place in the Larger Story. It is no accident that great movies include a hero, a villain, a betrayal, a battle to fight, a romance, and a beauty to rescue. It is The Epic Story and it is truer than anything we know. Adventure awaits. Listen.

Discover an experience that guides you on a journey into the one great Epic in which the Bible is set. These fun and provocative studies explore four films, each with two small-group meetings, *Dinner and a Movie* (Week 1), *Connecting the Dots* (Week 2), and an *Experience Guide* that offers valuable insights.

***Finding Jesus in the Movies* | 1574943553**
***Finding Redemption in the Movies* | 1574943421**
***Finding the Larger Story in Music* | 1574944207**

MORE.

In those rare moments of clarity we recognize that we want—no, need—more. Something inside us yearns for more from life, God, and Bible study than we've experienced. We sense we're more than we've become. We hope there's a lot more to God than we understand. And we need to believe there's more to the story than we've heard so far.

God dares us to desire more than a life of duty and obligation. Jesus didn't come to bring us more rules and regulations. He came to bring life (John 10:10) and invite us into a much larger story. Jesus referred to Isaiah 61:1-2 to describe His redemptive mission.

17 The scroll of the prophet Isaiah was handed to [Jesus]. Unrolling it, he found the place where it is written: 18 "The Spirit of the Lord is on me, because he has anointed me to preach good news to the poor. He has sent me to proclaim freedom for the prisoners and recovery of sight for the blind, to release the oppressed, 19 to proclaim the year of the Lord's favor."

LUKE 4:17-19, NIV

The MORE Series

The Larger Story into which we all were born is the greater, unseen reality that God reveals through Scripture and His Holy Spirit. This story includes perfect harmony and closeness dispelled by a failed insurrection ... the deadly fight between destroyer and redeemer ... paradise lost ... a beauty to be rescued ... the daring rescue in the dark of night ... ongoing dangerous battles ... final banishment of evil ... and the ultimate restoration of paradise. **Bible stories and teaching are set within the context of this larger backstory.**

Discovering God's truth from the Bible involves more than breaking verses down to their smallest parts and deconstructing a passage word-by-word. **The essence of the whole is more than the sum of its parts.** Traditional approaches to Bible study provide insight but can miss the magnificence of the forest while focusing on the trees. If we're not careful, we can drain the adventure and passion from Bible study and following Jesus, leaving us with details of duty and obligation.

God ... planted eternity in the human heart, but even so, people cannot see the whole scope of God's work from beginning to end.

ECCLESIASTES 3:11. NLT

Ecclesiastes explains why our hearts are moved by certain songs, dramatic movies, or stories. God has written eternity on our hearts so we resonate with its message. Jesus knew this and often used story to communicate because story is the language of the heart.

Larger Story Themes

DANGEROUS ADVENTURES

AN EPIC ROMANCE

VILLAINS & MONSTERS TO BE SLAIN

A BEAUTY TO BE RESCUED

BETRAYAL & INTRIGUE

BATTLES TO BE FOUGHT AND WON

UNEXPECTED TWISTS & TURNS

GOOD ULTIMATELY TRIUMPHS OVER EVIL

A HERO-REDEEMER

PARADISE RESTORED

The MORE Approach

Traditional Bible study methods break passages into their smallest parts to gain the insight and truth. There's some recognition of context (historical, literary, theological), but observation, interpretation, and application are seldom integrated with the Larger Story.

The key to the **MORE approach** is to start your study considering the elements of the Larger Story. Observation, interpretation, and application all emerge from the context of the Larger Story and lead toward heart transformation and life change here and now (Act III).

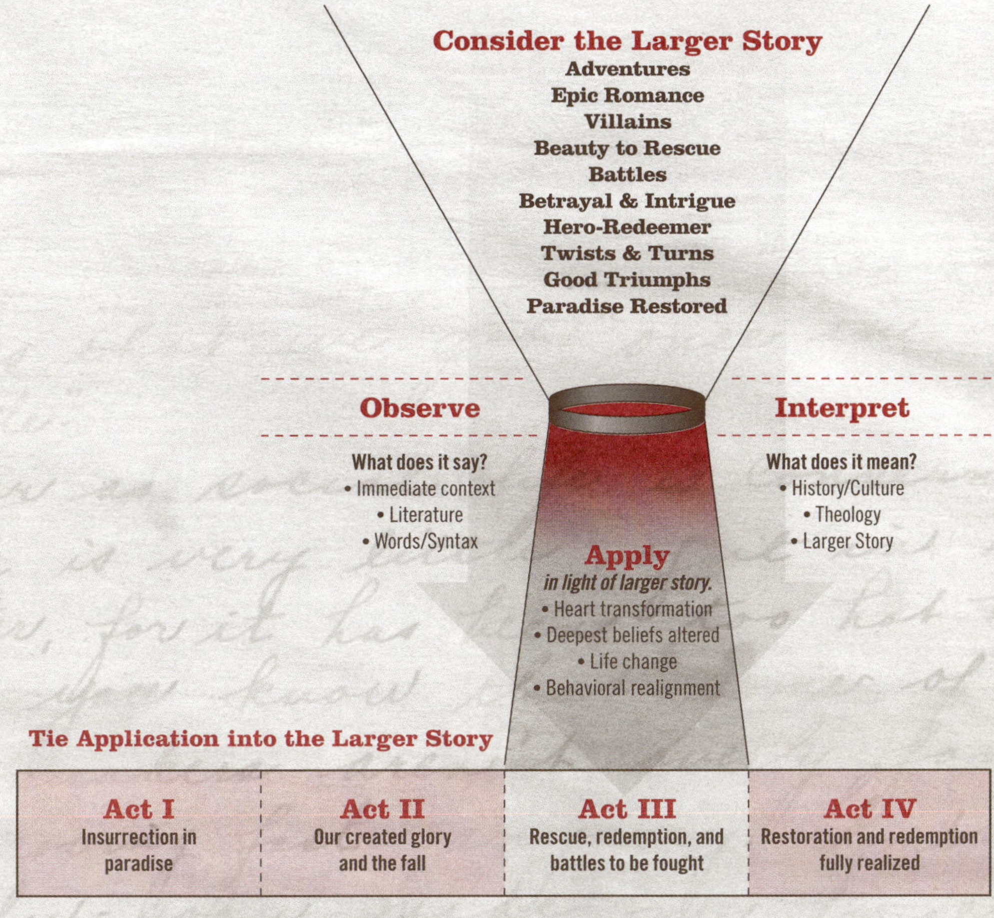

This approach will train you to look at the Bible and life from the perspective of the Larger Story—the eternity written on our hearts. **MORE acknowledges that story is the language of the heart and, without it, we can miss the wonder and power of the message.** Dare to discover and experience more of God, more of life, and more of your crucial role in the Great Adventure.

MARK

BEYOND THE RED LETTERS

The Book of Mark is to believers what any great action movie is to our culture … no holds barred, not wasted energy, intense and dynamic. In a fast-paced, fast-action style, Mark chronicles Jesus' daring rescue behind enemy lines amidst betrayal, intrigue, and unexpected twists and turns.

For so long Mark has been seen simply as one of the synoptics—a part of the Matthew, Mark, and Luke harmony—and his account is taken both as a part of the whole and as a reliable stand-alone testament of Jesus' ministry. While this approach is certainly a valid one, it dramatically understates the action teeming just underneath the surface; the epic battle between the Hero-Redeemer and the dark agents of the enemy always just beyond the red letters.

More than a small-group meeting and more than mere inductive analysis, **Mark: Beyond the Red Letters** has been created to guide you on an expedition into a magical realm where the unseen becomes seen—even if only for moments at a time—and the Larger Story that is being revealed by God takes the form of flesh and blood.

Larger Story Themes in Mark

Session 1: BACKSTORY – THE STAGE IS SET
Paradise; Insurrection; the Fall; Rescue; Restoration

Session 2: DANGEROUS ADVENTURE
Imposters; Earthquakes; Sinister plots: Be alert!

Session 3: A HERO REDEEMER
The time is now … "I am willing"

Session 4: A BEAUTY TO BE RESCUED
What do you want?

Session 5: BETRAYAL AND INTRIGUE
Where the seen and the unseen share the stage

Session 6: UNEXPECTED TWISTS AND TURNS
Our formulas thwarted

Session 7: GOOD ULTIMATELY TRIUMPHS OVER EVIL
… coming in the clouds with great power and glory

GROUP MEETING FLOW

OPENING SCENE

"Opening Scene" questions and experiences are designed to be fun and build community in your group. This helps put your group at ease and gets you talking casually about the day's topic. Everyone should participate so you can get to know one another and so you all can benefit from the diversity of stories and perspectives.

WHAT'S YOUR STORY?

Sharing your own story and listening to the stories of others will help you understand how your life fits into the Larger Story. Take time to discuss any key insights from take-home assignments, but focus on "Experience" or "Prep" as noted in each session.

BEHIND THE SCENES

"Behind the Scenes" sets the stage for continued discussions about the Larger Story as they unfold throughout the session. ***[LEADER: Invite volunteers to read various Scriptures throughout.]***

UNFOLDING THE LARGER STORY

This section opens your eyes to the Larger Story. Learn to see the truth of Scripture within the context of the Larger Story and then dare to question how your own story meshes with God's. As you embrace truth, you'll take steps toward a more passionate and personal relationship with God.

[LEADER: As a group, discuss as many questions as time permits. Be sure to highlight in advance the questions you don't want to miss. Try to keep things moving, but put the needs of group members ahead of completing an agenda.]

HEARTBEAT OF THE STORY

"Heartbeat" will help you connect with each other, with God, and especially with your own heart. A healthy small group should be a safe place for being open and real.

CONNECTING WITH MY STORY ...

Unique take-home assignments will lead you to go deeper with God and greatly enhance the overall experience of MORE.

SESSION ONE

DANGEROUS ADVENTURES
AN EPIC
ROMANCE
VILLAINS & MONSTERS TO BE SLAIN
A BEAUTY TO BE RESCUED
BETRAYAL & INTRIGUE
BATTLES TO BE FOUGHT AND WON
UNEXPECTED TWISTS & TURNS
GOOD ULTIMATELY TRIUMPHS OVER EVIL
A HERO-REDEEMER
PARADISE RESTORED

BACKSTORY–THE STAGE IS SET

BEYOND THE RED LETTERS

[6]John wore a camel-hair habit, tied at the waist with a leather belt. He ate locusts and wild field honey. [7]As he preached he said, "The real action comes next: The star in this drama, to whom I'm a mere stagehand, will change your life."

MARK 1:6-7, THE MESSAGE

They became very much afraid and said to one another, "Who then is this, that even the wind and the sea obey Him?"

MARK 4:41, NASB

LARGER STORY SYNOPSIS

Ours is a story of a daring rescue, a band of captives, uncertainty and intrigue, and a hero-redeemer sent by the one and only God.

The great stories capture our hearts because we catch a glimpse of our own epic in each of them. Scripture points out that God has placed eternity within our hearts (Ecclesiastes 3:11). It's the story of harmony manifested in Eden; of a betrayal that first wrecked universal harmony before the reality of paradise lost. It is the story of the one true king—the Hero Redeemer—sent on a daring rescue mission into enemy territory. The Larger Story of Mark identifies instances where the unseen world becomes visible in order to illuminate, even if only momentarily, a reality where the stakes are high, the ammo is live, and the danger is real.

OPTIONAL OPENING SCENE ON PAGE 112.

- PUT PEOPLE AT EASE
- ENCOURAGE PARTICIPATION

CAPTURE THE LIST ON A VISIBLE FLIP CHART OR POSTER PAGE.

OPENING SCENE

10-15 MINUTES

1. Take turns introducing yourself by naming your favorite action movie. You may broaden the field to include mysteries, adventure stories, and thrillers. Try to be specific in giving a couple of elements that makes this movie your favorite over others.

We use words like "gripping," "compelling," and "riveting" for a reason. We're all familiar with the stories that we like—even enjoy—but cannot be decribed with these words. Movie promoters and critics only use these or similar words to describe certain stories and movies.

2. What do you think makes some stories more compelling than others?

3. As a group, create a list of the elements common in the stories that intrigue us.

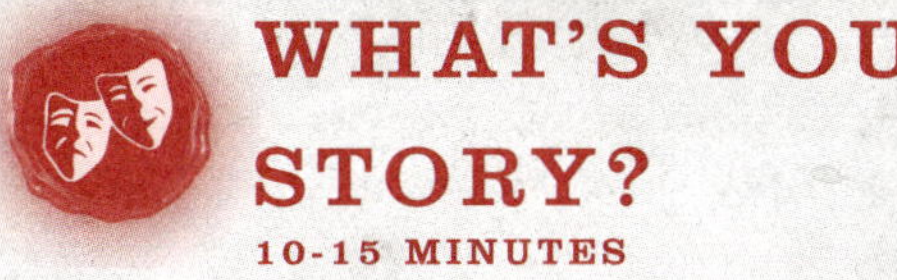

WHAT'S YOUR STORY?

10-15 MINUTES

Group Experience
- Divide into small sub-groups

Break into groups of 2-4 and talk about your story as a story of intrigue. Consider the list of common elements you just discussed. Identify a couple of these elements that you have experienced in your life. Take no more than five minutes, then reform the large group and create a short discussion.

1. In what ways has the story of your life resembled an action-adventure story of intrigue?

BEHIND THE SCENES

5-10 MINUTES

Most likely written first, Mark is the shortest of all the gospels and contains no resurrection appearances. The Greek found in Mark is inferior to that of other books of the New Testament. Among other things this may contribute to the hurried—almost frantic—pace felt in the action of Mark. The Book of Mark also includes many of what some have cited as the "hard sayings" of Jesus. Often this refers to troubling or difficult-to-discern passages. The sum of it is that down through the centuries Mark has traditionally been the least popular of the Gospels.

What we do know is that more than half of Jesus' recorded miracles appear here in Mark. Given that the word "immediately" appears more than forty times and this account of the life of Jesus cites the fewest words by Him, apparently the author of this Gospel was much more concerned with what Jesus ***did*** than what He ***said***.

Popularity, however, is not congruous with significance. Although scholars generally agree that Mark is not a biography, they differ on exactly how to distinguish the Gospel of Mark. Could it be more like the Book of Acts or maybe even a book of memoirs? Generally speaking, Mark does not fit neatly into any of our predefined categories. As a book, it is somewhat of a rogue. Regardless of where such scholarly conversations land, there is little doubt that among the Gospels Mark is The Epic. It is the "Lights, Camera, Action" of the New Testament. The Book of Mark is the Gospel of the Larger Story.

1. When you think of the grandest of stories, what attributes make these stories so much larger?

2. Considering what you know of the life of Jesus, what aspects of His life are consistent with the stories you mentioned in response to question 1 above?

"What we do in life, echoes in eternity."
*from **Gladiator***

The Larger Story that God continues to reveal finds its origins before Genesis 1:1. In the time before time there was harmony in the heavenly realm between the God and the angels. But jealousy and betrayal ushered in an era of discord and chaos. As Genesis begins and the Spirit hovers over the expanse, the rebellious events have only just concluded. True to His heart, God again creates harmony in Eden. And what happens next? Again betrayal leads to discord and chaos. Adam and Eve are expelled in order to be saved from eternal separation. But what does God do? God sets into motion a daring rescue into enemy territory.

3. As a group, briefly discuss the ways God has been at work throughout our history to reconcile us to Himself.

THE LARGER STORY IS NOT ABOUT PROPOSITION, FORMULA, OR SYSTEMS, IT IS ABOUT THE CRUCIAL ROLE YOU HAVE BEEN CALLED TO PLAY. IT IS ABOUT THE INVITATION INTO THE ADVENTURE.

Take a moment to discuss how the sense of urgency found in Mark may serve as a way to peek behind the curtain and into the Larger Story.

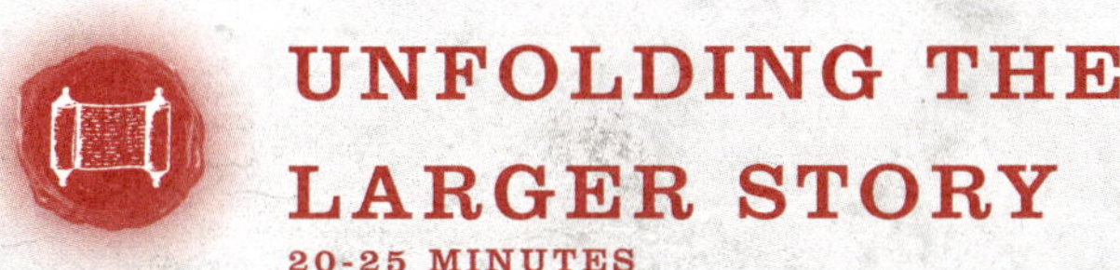

UNFOLDING THE LARGER STORY

20-25 MINUTES

The Larger Story that began in the age before time and will conclude in absolute restoration can be broken down into four acts. Before discovering the Larger Story elements in Mark let's first get acquainted with what we mean by Larger Story.

Act I: Insurrection in Paradise

> *... God is in the heavens; He does whatever He pleases.*
>
> **PSALM 115:3, NASB**

LOGOS
THE GREEK WORD LOGOS TRANSLATED "WORD" COULD ALSO MEAN "STORY." IT CONVEYS REVEALING AN IDEA, TALE, OR NARRATIVE. JESUS EMBODIES THE LOGOS OR LARGER STORY.

[1]In the beginning was the Word, and the
Word was with God, and the Word was God.
[2]He was in the beginning with God. [3]All
things were made through Him, and without
Him nothing was made that was made. [4]In
Him was life, and the life was the light of
men. [5]And the light shines in the darkness,
and the darkness did not comprehend it.

JOHN 1:1-5, NKJV

Find the following passages and, based on what you find, try to describe what this perfect harmony in the heavens must have been like.

ASK VOLUNTEERS TO FIND AND READ THESE VERSES.

Isaiah 11:9
Isaiah 65:17-25
Revelation 21:1-4
Revelation 22:1-5

The word Lucifer has also been translated as "Day Star" or "Morning Star" meaning "bearer of light." The name Lucifer does not appear elsewhere in the KJV and does not appear at all in more modern translations of the Bible.
from Wayne Grudem's ***Systematic Theology.***

But harmony was not sustained. All great stories must have a villain.

"How you are fallen from heaven, O Lucifer, son of the morning! How you are cut down to the ground, You who weakened the nations!

ISAIAH 14:12, NKJV

[15]From the day of your creation you were sheer
perfection . . . and then imperfection—evil!—
was detected in you. [16]In much buying and
selling you turned violent, you sinned! I threw
you, disgraced, off the mountain of God. I threw
you out—you, the anointed angel-cherub. ...
[17]Your beauty went to your head. You corrupted
wisdom by using it to get worldly fame. I threw
you to the ground, sent you sprawling before an
audience of kings and let them gloat over your
demise.

EZEKIEL 28:14-17, THE MESSAGE

OBSERVE

1. What flaws contributed to Lucifer's rebellion?

2. What makes this rebellion particularly heinous?

INTERPRET

Act II: Our Created Glory and the Fall

Traditionally, there has been much said about Original Sin and the subsequent fall of humanity. In these conversations, total depravity has been the order of the day. And while our fall and the notion of total depravity are absolutely true, perhaps these events do not represent what is truest about us. Also true is that we are God's image bearers, created in an original glory. Our creation and subsequent fall from grace both take place in Act II of the Larger Story.

ASK VOLUNTEERS TO READ THESE VERSES ALOUD.

[26]Then God said, "Let Us make man in Our
image, according to Our likeness. They will
rule the fish of the sea, the birds of the sky, the
animals, all the earth, and the creatures that
crawl on the earth." [27]So God created man in
His own image; He created him in the image of
God; He created them male and female. [28]God
blessed them.

GENESIS 1:26-28, HCSB

[1]Now the serpent was the most cunning of all
the wild animals that the LORD God had made.
He said to the woman, "Did God really say, 'You
can't eat from any tree in the garden'?" [2]The
woman said to the serpent, "We may eat the
fruit from the trees in the garden. But about the
fruit of the tree in the middle of the garden, God
said, 'You must not eat it or touch it, or you will
die.'" [4]"No! You will not die," the serpent said to
the woman.

GENESIS 3:1-4, HCSB

OBSERVE

3. At this point, how many Larger Story participants or players can you identify?

INTERPRET

4. If the expulsion of Adam and Eve from Eden was **not** totally punitive, then why do you think God would have felt it necessary to remove them from the garden of Eden?

HAD ADAM AND EVE EATEN FROM THE TREE OF LIFE AFTER EATING FROM THE TREE OF KNOWLEDGE IT WOULD HAVE MEANT ETERNAL SEPARATION FROM GOD. HE CAN BEAR BETRAYAL. HE CAN BEAR SIN. HE'S GOT IT COVERED. BUT WHAT GOD CAN ABSOLUTELY NOT BEAR IS ETERNAL SEPARATION FROM US, HIS BELOVED.

We know that we are of God, and the whole world is under the sway of the evil one.

1 JOHN 5:19, HCSB

First John 5:19 given above looks forward to Act III—the world in which we live and breathe.

Act III: Rescue, Redemption, and Battles to be Fought

ASK VOLUNTEERS TO READ THESE VERSES.

You have captured my heart, my sister, my bride. You have captured my heart with one glance of your eyes, with one jewel of your necklace.

SONG OF SONGS 4:9, HCSB

[17]The scroll of the prophet Isaiah was given to Him, and unrolling the scroll, He found the place where it was written: [18]The Spirit of the Lord is on Me, because He has anointed Me to preach good news to the poor. He has sent Me to proclaim freedom to the captives and recovery of sight to the blind, to set free the oppressed.

LUKE 4:17-18, HCSB

6. In the Larger Story, who is the "beauty to be rescued"?

OBSERVE

7. Describe the mission of the Hero-Redeemer.

And we know that God causes all things to work together for good to those who love God.

ROMANS 8:28, NASB

8. What does Romans 8:28 say about redemption? According to this passage, what does God cause–and what does He not cause?

INTERPRETATION

[3]For although we are walking in the flesh, we do not wage war in a fleshly way, [4]since the weapons of our warfare are not fleshly.

2 CORINTHIANS 10:3-4, HCSB

Be sober! Be on the alert! Your adversary the Devil is prowling around like a roaring lion, looking for anyone he can devour.

1 PETER 5:8, HCSB

9. Where do you think the Villain may be found today?

PERSONAL APPLICATION

10. Ultimately, what do you think the battle mentioned in 2 Corinthians 10:3 is over?

Guard your heart above all else, for it is the source of life.
Proverbs 4:23

Act IV: Restoration and Redemption Fully Realized

ASK A VOLUNTEER TO READ ROMANS 8:18-23

That's why I don't think there's any comparison between the present hard times and the coming good times. The created world itself can hardly wait for what's coming next. Everything in creation is being more or less held back. God reins it in until both creation and all the creatures are ready and can be released at the same moment into the glorious times ahead. Meanwhile, the joyful anticipation deepens. All around us we observe a pregnant creation. The difficult times of pain throughout the world

> *are simply birth pangs. But it's not only around us; it's within us. The Spirit of God is arousing us within. We're also feeling the birth pangs. These sterile and barren bodies of ours are yearning for full deliverance.*
>
> ***ROMANS 8:18-23, THE MESSAGE***

> *"Now concerning that day or hour no one knows—neither the angels in heaven nor the Son—except the Father.*
>
> ***MARK 13:32, HCSB***

"I will see you again ... but not yet. Not yet."
*from **Gladiator***

According to the Scripture, even creation anxiously awaits the day of ultimate redemption. One translation describes creation as groaning as it waits to be released into its own glory. But about that day we can only wait. We only know "not yet." Jesus Himself didn't even know.

11. In what ways do you sense the building drama of ultimate and final redemption?

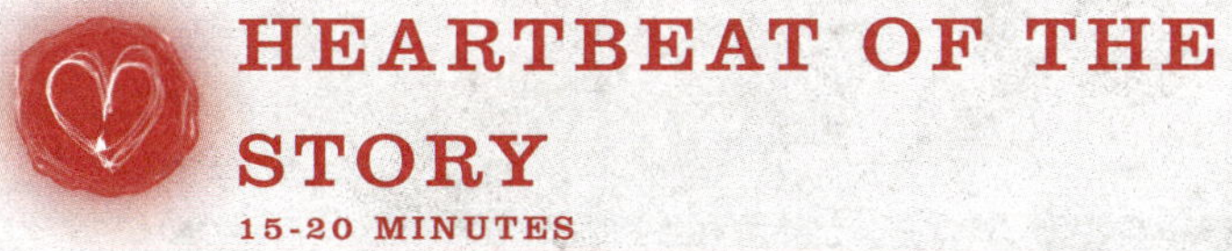

HEARTBEAT OF THE STORY

15-20 MINUTES

1. Bambi was "twitterpated." Rose's face flushed aboard ***Titanic.*** When have you felt the most in love?

2. If a hero could swoop in and rescue you, from what would you want to be rescued? Rank the following categories according to need.

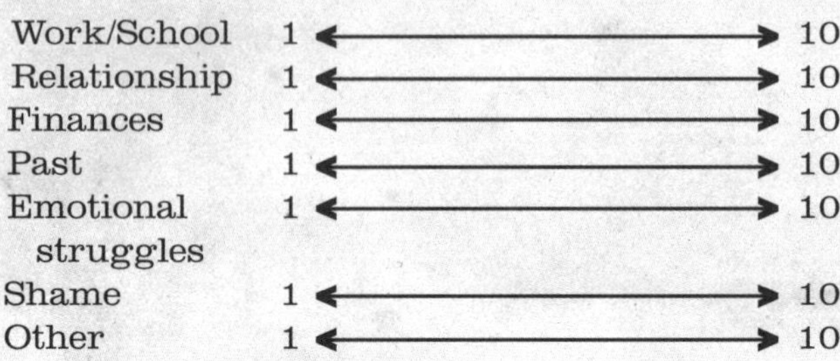

Work/School	1	⟷	10
Relationship	1	⟷	10
Finances	1	⟷	10
Past	1	⟷	10
Emotional struggles	1	⟷	10
Shame	1	⟷	10
Other	1	⟷	10

3. When you think about the Larger Story, how do you feel?
   - ❒ I'm playing my part and absorbed in the plot.
   - ❒ I'm an extra and wonder if I'm going to get eliminated from the script.
   - ❒ I'm a spectator.
   - ❒ The Larger Story isn't my story.
   - ❒ Other ____________

4. How does your answer to question 3 make you feel?

Any conversation about the Larger Story must include the crucial role we all have been called to play. There are many tools available to us ranging from spiritual gift surveys to personality profiles to character types (maybe some of you have been told what animal best represents who you are). Regardless of which of these tools you have used, will decide to use, or will never use, make no mistake about it—you have a standing invitation to the adventure of life with God. But more than that, you have been created to fill a specific role.

As you take the next step to discovering the inner-workings and intrigue of the Larger Story, here are some points to keep in mind:

Father! All things are possible for You. Take this cup away from Me. Nevertheless, not what I will, but what you will ... But Jesus let out a loud cry and breathed His last.

MARK 14:36; 15:37, HCSB

• The adventure of the Larger Story is full of unexpected twists and turns. Surprise and intrigue await around every corner and behind every decision.

5. How do you feel about being left with no working formulas?

[12]Immediately the Spirit drove Him into the wilderness. [13]He was in the wilderness 40 days, being tempted by Satan. He was with the wild animals ...

MARK 1:12-13, HCSB

• The Larger Story is not necessarily the safest place to be. And there is no guarantee of God's intervention. Our only guarantee is God's redemption.

6. Does the "No Guaranteed Intervention Policy" leave you a little unsettled? Does the prospect of danger make the Larger Story more or less appealing?

Moved with compassion, Jesus reached out His hand and touched him. "I am willing," He told him. "Be made clean."

MARK 1:41, HCSB

• Like every great story, the Larger Story has a hero, too. The power of our Hero-Redeemer causes the spiritual and physical realms to collide. He is both cunning and powerful. He is both humble servant and commanding general.

7. What sort of Hero-Redeemer do you think the Larger Story requires?

When the scribes of the Pharisees saw that He was eating with sinners and tax collectors, they asked His disciples, "Why does He eat with tax collectors and sinners?" [17]When Jesus heard this, He told them, "Those who are well don't need a doctor, but the sick do need one. I didn't come to call the righteous, but sinners."

MARK 2:16-17, HCSB

• There is a beauty to be rescued and that beauty is you. Understanding the Larger Story requires you to consider metaphorical allusions that are unfamiliar. God doesn't just tolerate you. Believe it or not, God is actually smitten with you.

8. Is it hard for you to use a word like "smitten" when describing how God feels about you? If yes, then why do you think that is?

[9]"Therefore, what will the owner of the vineyard do? He will come and destroy the farmers and give the vineyard t others. [10]Haven't you read this Scripture: The stone that the builders rejected has become the cornerstone. [11]This came from the Lord and is wonderful in our eyes?"

MARK 12:9-11, HCSB

• Although we know that in the Larger Story good ultimately triumphs over evil, this victory does not come without a fight. This triumph requires our participation in a battle that is very real. Into this breech of battle is our calling.

9. Describe some of the battles in which you are currently engaged. Talk a little about the differences between Larger Story battles and small story battles.

> *[10]Since He had healed many, all who had diseases were pressing toward Him to touch Him. [11]Whenever the unclean spirits saw Him, those possessed fell down before Him and cried out, "You are the Son of God!" [12]And He would strongly warn them not to make Him known.*
>
> ***MARK 3:10-12, HCSB***

• There is an unseen realm of our reality that is both real and dangerous. There is a certain enemy with minions. Often in Mark these two worlds collide in the presence of Jesus. The Larger Story is chocked full of betrayal and intrigue. There are many secrets.

10. How does the notion of an unseen reality affect you?

Connect with Your Story This Week

The take-home activities will greatly enhance your MORE experience. The "Reflection" assignments are most important for this week.

CONNECTING WITH MY STORY

REFLECTION

Between now and your next session, read the Gospel of Mark through the lens of the Larger Story. Try to do this in one sitting. Set aside 90 uninterrupted minutes.

Option: Assign portions of the 16 chapters of Mark to sub-groups of 2-3

Some suggestions for seeing the Gospel differently:
- Read Mark silently with the exception of Jesus' words. Read His words aloud (in many Bibles, His words appear in red ink).
- Listen to Mark using an audio Bible of some kind.

One way to determine the crucial role you have been called to play in the Larger Story is by paying attention to what moves you. Often our hearts recognize God's invitation to us through our own stories. As you read or listen, jot down words, phrases, or verses that stick out. Use the boxes below to sort what moves you into its Larger Story context.

Dangerous Adventure

A Beauty to be Rescued

Betrayal and Intrigue

Unexpected Twists and Turns

Good Triumphs over Evil

A Hero-Redeemer

SESSION TWO

DANGEROUS ADVENTURES

AN EPIC ROMANCE

VILLAINS & MONSTERS TO BE SLAIN

A BEAUTY TO BE RESCUED

BETRAYAL & INTRIGUE

BATTLES TO BE FOUGHT AND WON

UNEXPECTED TWISTS & TURNS

GOOD ULTIMATELY TRIUMPHS OVER EVIL

A HERO-REDEEMER

PARADISE RESTORED

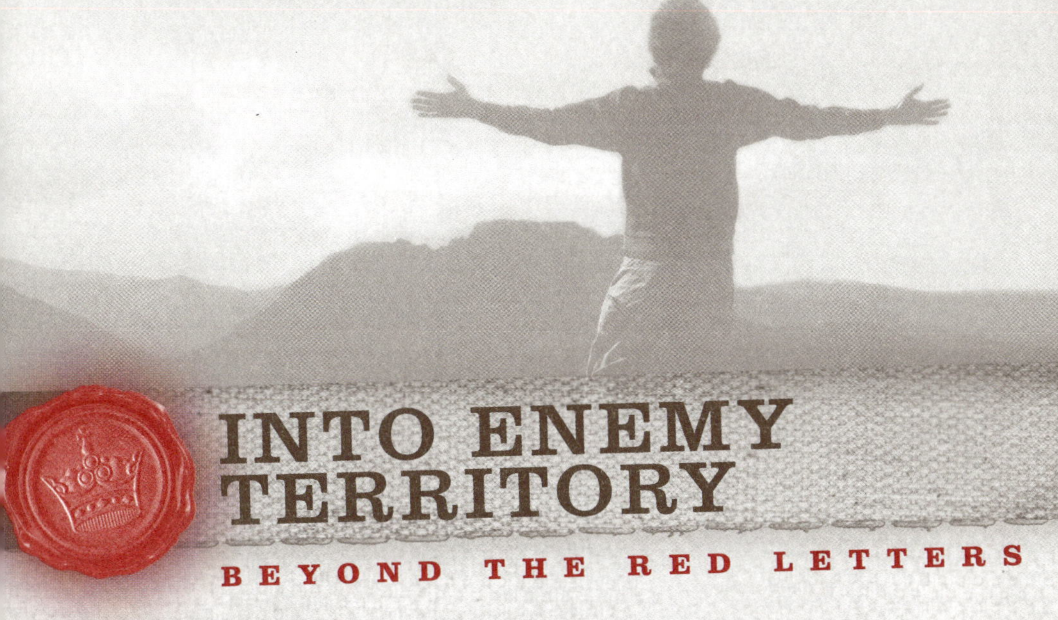

INTO ENEMY TERRITORY

BEYOND THE RED LETTERS

"Do not think that I came to bring peace on earth. I did not come to bring peace but a sword.

MATTHEW 10:34, NKJV

Immediately the Pharisees went out and started plotting with the Herodians against Him, how they might destroy Him.

MARK 3:6, HCSB

LARGER STORY SYNOPSIS

Every great story is set on the grandest of stages where danger is the order of the day and safety is no longer an option.

By Mark 1:10 the heavens have been "torn open", the Spirit has descended into our world, and God's voice has announced the insertion of the Hero into enemy territory. This daring rescue mission is a path fraught with perils both physical and spiritual. Although Jesus has forfeited a portion of His power, He has at His disposal various weapons to negotiate His mission. The Larger Story is not a place of safety. It is not a mission for the fainthearted. But we, too, have weapons at our disposal as we accept the invitation to join God in His redemptive pursuits.

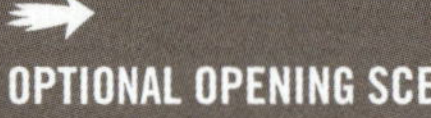

OPTIONAL OPENING SCENE ON PAGE 114.

OPENING SCENE

10-15 MINUTES

Perhaps the most compelling element of the Larger Story is the dangerous adventure. The great stories of our culture have in common the ability to capture us right from the start. We instinctively sense that the stakes are high and the danger real.

1. Which of these beginnings excites you most? Least? Using a scale of one to five (five being highest) rank each beginning.
   ____ When you buckle your seat belt before you pull out of the driveway on vacation
   ____ When the lights fade before the motion picture begins
   ____ When the brakes are released on a roller coaster
   ____ When the binding crackles as you open a new book
   ____ When the alarm clock buzzes on the first day of a new job
   ____ When the orchestra finishes tuning and the conductor counts off the overture
   ____ When your pager vibrates and your restaurant table is ready
   ____ When you rush to your couch because "Lost" or "24" is coming on
   ____ When the gun is fired to start a road race
   ____ When the music crescendos marking the beginning of worship

2. What opening scenes from literature or the movies do you remember best? Which ones would you read or watch over and over again?

3. Describe an event that set into motion a memorable adventure for you. Talk about why you remember this event. Was there something about this event that made you come alive?

4. Give some reasons for avoiding danger. Why do you think God would invite you into a dangerous adventure? Or would He?

WHAT'S YOUR STORY

10-15 MINUTES

Last week you were asked to review the Book of Mark as part of the Reflection exercise given in Connecting with My Story. Part of the exercise included citing those instances that had the most profound impact on you.

Take turns revealing your internal world in the following way:

- Share with the group one of these instances.
- To what aspect of the Larger Story did you assign this event?

Do your best to articulate why these specific events, words, or circumstances moved you.

Most stories begin "in medias res", in the middle of the action. The author, screenwriter, or playwright throws you into a situation. This technique captures your attention, boosts your pulse rate, and causes you to ask questions. You're involved. You're invested.

The Gospel According to Mark begins "in medias res:"

- **Supernatural warriors have been dispatched.**
- **The Villain has ordered the execution of children.**
- **A young couple is hunted by a dark lord.**

BEHIND THE SCENES

5-10 MINUTES

There are many places that allow us a glimpse into the backstory of Jesus' dangerous enterprise. It embodies all the ingredients of the perfect plan: cunning, planning, patience, risk.

ASK VOLUNTEERS TO READ THESE VERSES TO THE GROUP.

And I will put enmity between [the serpent] and the woman, and between your offspring and hers; he will crush your head, and you will strike his heel."

GENESIS 3:15, NIV

Genesis 3:15 has been referred to as the proto-gospel and is the forerunner to the Gospels of the New Testament. This is the first mention of ultimate redemption made possible by Jesus in that He is an offspring of a human that will strike the final, fatal blow to Satan—albeit not before Satan has inflicted his own wounds.

OBSERVE

1. What does the early disclosure of Genesis 3:15 reveal to you about the nature of Jesus' mission?

God's wisdom is something mysterious that goes deep into the interior of his purposes. You don't find it lying around on the surface. It's not the latest message, but more like the oldest—what God determined as the way to bring out his best in us, long before we ever arrived on the scene. The experts of our day haven't a clue about what this eternal plan is. If they had, they wouldn't have killed the Master of the God-designed life on a cross.

1 CORINTHIANS 2:7-8, THE MESSAGE

2. Read 1 Corinthians 2:7-8 and talk about the mysteries inherent in the adventure of the Larger Story. What do you think this says about the dangerous adventure we're invited into?

Thousands of years of Scripture pull back the curtain, moment-to-moment, to give us fleeting revelations of the shimmering world on the other side of reality where God has been, and continues to be, at work. Take a look at the pairs of verses below. The first is an Old Testament prophesy. This is followed by a New Testament account.

ASK FOR VOLUNTEERS TO READ EACH OF THESE SETS.

Bethlehem Ephrathah, you are small among the clans of Judah; One will come from you to be ruler over Israel for Me. His origin is from antiquity, from eternity.

MICAH 5:2, HCSB

After Jesus was born in Bethlehem of Judea in the days of King Herod, wise men from the east arrived unexpectedly in Jerusalem,

MATTHEW 2:1, HCSB

Therefore, the Lord Himself will give you a sign: The virgin will conceive, have a son, and name him Immanuel.

ISAIAH 7:14, HCSB

[26]In the sixth month, the angel Gabriel was sent by God to a town in Galilee called Nazareth, [27]to a virgin engaged to a man named Joseph, of the house of David. The virgin's name was Mary.

LUKE 1:26-27, HCSB

*"Throw it to the potter," the Lord said to me—
this magnificent price I was valued by them.
So I took the 30 pieces of silver and threw it
into the house of the Lord, to the potter.*

ZECHARIAH 11:13, HCSB

*14 Then one of the Twelve—the man called
Judas Iscariot—went to the chief priests 15 and
said, "What are you willing to give me if I
hand Him over to you?" So they weighed out
30 pieces of silver for him.*

MATTHEW 26:14-15, HCSB

Even my friend in whom I trusted, one who ate my bread, has lifted up his heel against me.

PSALM 41:9, HCSB

*3 Then Satan entered Judas, called Iscariot, who
was numbered among the Twelve. 4 He went
away and discussed with the chief priests and
temple police how he could hand Him over to
them.*

LUKE 22:3-4, HCSB

3. What sort of emotions does this glimpse behind the curtain stir within you?

4. In what ways do these prophesies change the way you think about the Book of Mark? How do they open your eyes to the Larger Story and the dangerous adventure that has been unfolding throughout Act III?

UNFOLDING THE LARGER STORY

20-25 MINUTES

Into the Wild

To be on mission with God is to take the first step into the wild. It's an untamed land where surprise is the rule and the fantastic is commonplace. Once past the proverbial Rubicon the adventurer discovers that this world is a two-sided one with danger on both sides of the line dividing the physical world from the spiritual one. The adventure begins here.

"Crossing the Rubicon" is an expression finding its origins in an Italian river. The expression means "past the point of no return." In an act of war, Julius Caesar crossed the river several years before Christ purportedly having said, "the die is cast."

And He was in the wilderness forty days being tempted by Satan; and He was with the wild beasts

MARK 1:13, NASB

ASK A VOLUNTEER TO READ MARK 1:13.

1. Describe a time when you sensed the supernatural at work around you. What did it feel like? What were the signs?

INTERPRET

As soon as He came up out of the water, He saw the heavens being torn open and the Spirit descending to Him...

MARK 1:10, HCSB

ASK A VOLUNTEER TO READ MARK 1:10.

2. Assuming that the sky was literally "torn open," what are the story implications?

PERSONAL APPLICATION

3. What is it about the dangerous adventure that transcends the smaller stories you find yourself in? Why do you think the dangerous adventure of the Larger Story is so captivating?

4. Why do you think the Villain of the Larger Story would attempt to draw you into the smaller stories of life? Why do you think we are so vulnerable to these schemes?

Jon Krakauer's book *Into the Wild* describes a young man, Chris McCandless, who forsakes all the trappings of life in favor of a life in the wilderness of Alaska. Krakauer concludes that McCandless and others like him are driven by the question, "Do I have what it takes?"

Danger on Every Side

5 After looking around at them with anger and sorrow at the hardness of their hearts, He told the man, "Stretch out your hand." So he stretched it out, and his hand was restored. 6 Immediately the Pharisees went out and started plotting with the Herodians against Him, how they might destroy Him.

MARK 3:5-6, HCSB

7 And he cried out with a loud voice, "What do You have to do with me, Jesus, Son of the Most High God? I beg You before God, don't torment me!" 8 For He had told him, "Come out of the man, you unclean spirit!" 9 "What is your name?" He asked him. "My name is Legion," he answered Him, "because we are many."

MARK 5:7-9, HCSB

5. Describe the dangers represented in Mark 3:5-6 and 5:7-9. What do you think makes these accounts Larger Story events as opposed to smaller story plots?

Small stories ... our individual stories, birth to death, in the seen realm where the main plot is about us–you– and you are the central character.

Larger Story ... the story that has been in motion since eternity in both the seen and unseen realms; where we each have a part to play and the plot is bigger than we are; a reality where the stakes are much higher.

Peril in the Womb of Time

Many leaders are going to show up with forged identities claiming, 'I'm the One.' They will deceive a lot of people. When you hear of wars and rumored wars, keep your head and don't panic. This is routine history, and no sign of the end. Nation will fight nation and ruler fight ruler, over and over. Earthquakes will occur in various places. There will be famines. But these things are nothing compared to what's coming. "And watch out! They're going to drag you into court. And then it will go from bad to worse, dog-eat-dog, everyone at your throat because you carry my name. You're placed there as sentinels to truth.

MARK 13:6-9, THE MESSAGE

6. What does the passage from the Book of Mark above tell you about what to expect once engaged in the Larger Story?

OBSERVE

7. What do you think this reveals about your role in the Larger Story?

INTERPRET

... And Undisputed Champion

The Lord is a warrior; Yahweh is His name.
EXODUS 15:3, HCSB

But now, GOD'S Message, the God who made you in the first place, Jacob, the One who got you started, Israel: "Don't be afraid, I've redeemed you. I've called your name. You're mine."
ISAIAH 43:1, THE MESSAGE

8. Filtered through the verses above, how do you think we should confront whatever fears we may have regarding our place in the Larger Story?

Now we know the players and we are aware of the crucial role God has given us in His Larger Story. There is a Villain with minions and a Hero-Redeemer that has called us to His side. As we take our own steps into the wild we will most certainly draw the fire—if not from THE Villain, then from his minions.

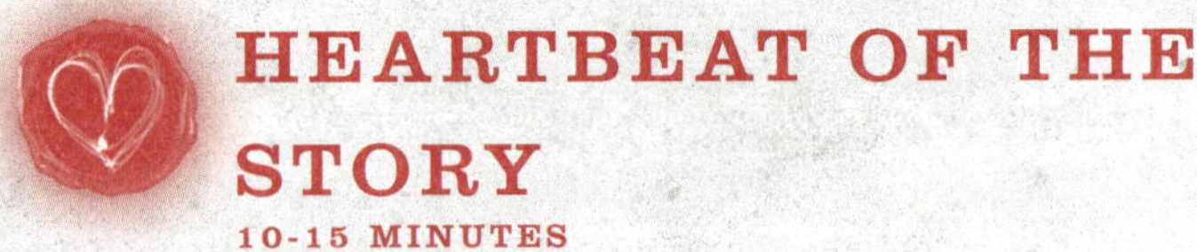

1. In what ways is the dangerous adventure described here frightening to you?

2. As you think about the Larger Story, your crucial role, and the imminent peril, what specific part of your life comes to mind?

Fear typically comes from one of two places: our desire for control or a desire to avoid failure. Usually our behaviors, not our words, are indicative of what we believe in the deepest places of our heart. Psalm 51:6 tells us that God desires truth in the inmost being.

3. When assessing your fears, what could they indicate about what you REALLY believe?

4. As you assess the deepest places of who you are, what do you think might hinder your efforts to accept God's invitation to join Him in the redemptive adventure?

I looked up and there before me was a man dressed in linen, with a belt of the finest gold around his waist. His body was like chrysolite, his face like lightning, his eyes like flaming torches, his arms and legs like the gleam of burnished bronze, and his voice like the sound of a multitude.

DANIEL 10:5–6, NIV

Host: This word implies a mass of soldiers organized for war at an appointed time. Too often when we think of angels, we think of cherubs, a cartoon Cupid, or Monica from "Touched by an Angel". Daniel's depiction is much closer. We should think Navy SEALs, Roman Centurions, or Arthur's knights, not harp playing, toga wearing, cloud floating children.

"You alone are the LORD.
You have made the heavens,
The heaven of heavens with all their host,
The earth and all that is on it,
The seas and all that is in them.
You give life to all of them
And the heavenly host bows down before You.

NEHEMIAH 9:6, NASB

Briefly discuss the fears that have been mentioned as they relate to the passages above.

Group Prayer

Close this MORE experience by asking God to reveal the crucial role He has for each member. Ask Him to make us aware of the hosts that surround us as we stand on the precipice of the great adventure of a life with Him.

Connecting with Your Story This Week

Allocate some time this week for Connecting with My Story. This week's Reflection will focus on the role you are called into as God continues to reveal the Larger Story of redemption.

CONNECTING WITH MY STORY THIS WEEK

Jesus replied, "No one who puts his hand to the plow and looks back is fit for the service in the kingdom of God."

LUKE 9:62, NIV

The words of Scripture are only representative of the cosmic circumstance and backstory that includes both the physical and spiritual, the seen and the unseen, and everything in between. The words breathe and expand. They point us in the direction of the Larger Story.

This week's Reflection is a journaling exercise intended to allow time for you to ask God about the role you have been called to play in the Larger Story. Read the verse above, close your eyes, and imagine standing on the threshold of something great—your great adventure. It is the point beyond which we do not look back, only forward. For Chris McCandless in *Into the Wild* this occurs as he stands on the edge of the Alaskan wilderness knowing that his next step will take him beyond the self-imposed line of no-return. You may also consider taking an evening and watching an epic movie like *Gladiator*, *Braveheart*, *Star Wars*, *Lord of the Rings*, or even *Seabiscuit* with other group members. Use the space below to journal your thoughts as you consider the defining moment of accepting the invitation.

Use the following questions as a guide.

How have I been uniquely created?
What makes my heart come alive?
What fears stand between me and the adventure that awaits?
Where do I sense God to be most active in the world around me?
What do I enjoy most about my spiritual life?

SESSION THREE

DANGEROUS ADVENTURES
AN EPIC
ROMANCE
VILLAINS & MONSTERS
TO BE SLAIN
A BEAUTY TO BE
RESCUED
BETRAYAL & INTRIGUE
BATTLES TO BE FOUGHT
AND WON
UNEXPECTED
TWISTS & TURNS
GOOD ULTIMATELY TRIUMPHS OVER EVIL
A HERO-REDEEMER
PARADISE
RESTORED

A FORCE OF NATURE

BEYOND THE RED LETTERS

For even the Son of Man did not come to be served, but to serve, and to give His life—a ransom for many."

MARK 10:45, HCSB

[11]Whenever the unclean spirits saw Him, they would fall down before Him and shout, "You are the Son of God!" [12]And He earnestly warned them not to tell who He was.

MARK 3:11-12, NASB

LARGER STORY SYNOPSIS

All the great stories boast a hero with superior knowledge, unprecedented skill, and other-worldly power.

The archetypical hero almost universally possesses the same attributes: great strength and power, incredible persuasion, keen awareness, sacrificial leadership, and cunning. Think *Lord of the Rings* or practically any Disney movie that's ever been made. In these cases the story includes a transformation of sorts. The Hero Redeemer of the Larger Story embodies all of the aspects of the Hero in addition to the willingness to mock evil. Jesus the Son of God is not only the centerpiece of the Epic in which we live and breathe, but also the Larger Story of the unseen realm.

OPENING SCENE

10-15 MINUTES

1. Who are the great heroes of our culture—either fictitious or not? What makes these men and women great in your eyes?

To open this session of *Beyond the Red Letters* we're going to watch a clip from the movie *Gladiator*. In this scene you'll see Maximus in action during his first appearance on Rome's grandest stage: the Coliseum. For those unfamiliar with the whole story, *Gladiator* chronicles Maximus' journey from a commanding general that became a slave; from a slave that became a gladiator; a gladiator that defied an empire.

Show clip from *Gladiator* (Chapter 16, see page 115 for instructions).

2. What strikes you as particularly inspiring about this scene? What attributes does Maximus possess?

My name is Maximus Decimus Meridius, commander of the armies of the north. General to the Felix Legions, loyal servant to the true emperor, Marcus Aurelius. Father to a murdered son, husband to a murdered wife. And I will have my vengeance, in this life or the next.
from ***Gladiator***

3. How do you think the heroes or our culture (or the heroes of your life) relate to the Hero Redeemer of the Larger Story? Do they share the same mission? Do they work in tandem?

4. Take a few minutes to discuss why you think some people are able to rise above others? What makes them unique?

WHAT'S YOUR STORY

10-15 MINUTES

1. Where do you think our culture's fascination with heroes comes from?

2. What heroic qualities do you most admire?
   - ❒ Self-sacrifice
   - ❒ Awareness of the need
   - ❒ Dignity
   - ❒ Justice
   - ❒ Decisiveness
   - ❒ Courage
   - ❒ Integrity
   - ❒ Cunning
   - ❒ Strength
   - ❒ Supernatural gifts
   - ❒ Lack of passivity
   - ❒ Accepting the call regardless of the cost
   - ❒ Other ___________________

The Hero's Journey

- The hero lives in his world
- The hero is summoned to adventure
- Leaving his world, the hero enters the unique world
- He is mentored and finds friends
- An enemy rises to challenge the hero
- The hero faces tests and trials
- Ultimately, the hero faces an epic ordeal against the enemy to receive a great reward
- The hero comes face-to-face with death and is resurrected
- The hero returns to his world a victor with a prize

May Parker: You'll never guess who he wants to be ... Spider-Man!
Peter Parker: Why?
May Parker: He knows a hero when he sees one. Too few characters out there, flying around like that, saving old girls like me. And Lord knows, kids like Henry need a hero. Courageous, self-sacrificing people. Setting examples for all of us. Everybody loves a hero. ... I believe there's a hero in all of us, that keeps us honest, gives us strength, makes us noble, and finally allows us to die with pride, even though sometimes we have to be steady, and give up the thing we want the most. Even our dreams.
from ***Spider-Man 2***

3. If you could have one of those qualities manifested in your own life today, which would you choose? What need in your life does that quality meet?

4. Do you think you're called to be one of the Larger Story heroes? Why or why not?

BEHIND THE SCENES
5-10 MINUTES

The Hero Redeemer of the Larger Story is perhaps best described as a force of nature. Those that have visited present-day Holy Land often remark on the feeling that results from walking in what may have been the same steps Jesus actually walked. This makes perfect sense once you take into account that Jesus is the force behind all created things. Most likely the creation is affected by its Creator in some way. As He walked we may assume that there was something like the wake a boat leaves in the water that rippled through time and space, its remnant remaining even today. (See John 1.)

Our Hero Redeemer is a special sort of entity that is both like and unlike any of those mentioned earlier. He is both God and man at once. He has power in both the seen and unseen world. The Italian word "sprezzatura" suggests the appearance of ease in accomplishing any task. Jesus demonstrates a certain "sprezzatura" as He moves in and out of the different elements of the Larger Story. He is the perfecter of our faith. The author of the Larger Story.

During this *Behind the Scenes*, take five to ten minutes to talk about the implications of Jesus' uniqueness.

Implications of the Deity of Christ
- Jesus makes it possible for us to know God.
- Ultimate redemption is available to us through Him.
- Through the deity of Jesus, a restored relationship between God and humanity is possible.
- Worship of Jesus is appropriate.

Implications of Jesus' humanity
- Jesus' death is truly atoning. His death makes it possible for Him to redeem all things.
- Because He has experienced human-ness we know He can sympathize with us.
- Jesus makes it possible for us to see the truest nature of humanity.
- God is not aloof and unconcerned, but near and engaged.
- To become human, Jesus voluntarily forfeited some aspects of His deity (Mk. 13:32, Phil. 2:5ff). For instance, He acknowledges that there are things He doesn't know.

1. What bearing do these implications have on the Larger Story?

"The man who yields to a particular temptation has not felt its full power. He has given in while the temptation has yet something in reserve. Only the man who does not yield to a temptation, who, as regards to that particular temptation, is sinless, knows the full extent of that temptation."
from Leon Morris' ***Lord from Heaven***

New Testament writers ascribe the term *kyrios* (Lord) to Jesus. *Kyrios* is the usual translation of the name Jehovah. For the Israelites, *kyrios* literally maintains equality between Jesus and the Father.

2. When you look beyond the red letters to the other side of the curtain, how has the role of the Hero Redeemer within this greater reality taken on new life for you?

I need a hero
Up where the
mountains meet
Out where
the lightning
strikes the sea I
can swear that
there's someone
somewhere
watching me
Through the wind
and the chill and
the rain and the
storm and the
flood I can feel his
approach like the
fire in my blood ...

From "Holding Out For A Hero"
Words and music by Dean Pitchford and James Richard Steinman (BMI)

3. Both Jesus' deity and His humanity point towards the notion of redemption (restoration, atonement). What is your understanding of redemption? How do you define "redemption"?

UNFOLDING THE LARGER STORY

20-25 MINUTES

The Author

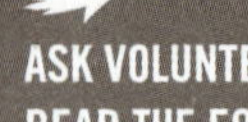

ASK VOLUNTEERS TO READ THE FOLLOWING VERSES.

[40]But He said to them, "Why are you so fearful?
How is it that you have no faith?" [41]And they
feared exceedingly, and said to one another,
"Who can this be, that even the wind and the sea
obey Him!"

MARK 4:40-41, NKJV

[25]A woman suffering from bleeding for 12
years [26]had endured much under many doctors.
She had spent everything she had and was not
helped at all. ... [27]Having heard about Jesus, she
came behind Him in the crowd and touched His

robe. ... [29]Instantly her flow of blood ceased,
and she sensed in her body that she was
cured .... [30]At once Jesus realized in Himself
that power had gone out from Him ... ."

MARK 5:25-27, 29-30, HCSB

[23]Just then there was a man in their
synagogue with an unclean spirit; and he
cried out, [24]saying, "What business do we have
with each other, Jesus of Nazareth? Have You
come to destroy us? I know who You are—the
Holy One of God!" [25]And Jesus rebuked him,
saying, "Be quiet, and come out of him!"

MARK 1:23-25, NASB

[13]And He sent two of His disciples and said to
them, "Go into the city, and a man will meet
you carrying a pitcher of water; follow him;
[14]and wherever he enters, say to the owner
of the house ... "Where is My guest room
in which I may eat the Passover with My
disciples?"' [15]"And he himself will show you a
large upper room furnished and ready; prepare
for us there."

MARK 14:13-15, NASB

OBSERVE

1. Over what areas of our known world do you think Jesus demonstrates mastery in these passages?

INTERPRET

2. How does this mastery contribute to His ability as the Hero Redeemer of the Larger Story?

PERSONAL APPLICATION

"The Spirit of the Lord is on Me … He has sent Me to proclaim freedom to the captives and recovery of sight to the blind."
Luke 4:18, HCSB

My people are broken—shattered!—and they put on band-aids, Saying, 'It's not so bad. You'll be just fine.' But things are not 'just fine'!
Jeremiah 6:14, The Message

3. In what ways is Jesus' power comforting?

4. In what ways do some of the circumstances described in these passages (sickness, demonic activity) leave you a little unsettled?

Super Hero Status

For even the Son of Man did not come to be served, but to serve, and to give His life—a ransom for many."

MARK 10:45, HCSB

5. What does Mark 10:45 reveal to you about your current condition?

6. What also does it say to you that it takes a Hero Redeemer with Jesus' attributes to release you?

*[13]"For from the least of them even to the
greatest of them, everyone is greedy for
gain, And from the prophet even to the priest
everyone deals falsely. [14]"They have healed
the brokenness of My people superficially,
Saying, 'Peace, peace,' But there is no peace."*

JEREMIAH 6:13-14, NASB

READ JEREMIAH 6:13-14 TO THE GROUP.

*[43] "And if your hand causes your downfall,
cut it off .... [45]And if your foot causes your
downfall, cut it off ... [47]And if your eye causes
your downfall, gouge it out.*

MARK 9:43,45,47, HCSB

7. What do you think the words of Jesus shown here in Mark 9 reveal about the significance of what ails us physically? If not for physical comfort, then what do you think the Hero Redeemer of the Larger Story has come to fight for?

There is a difference between knowing and believing. "Knowing" suggests an academic knowledge or mental assent while "believing" takes place more within the core of who we are—"believing" is commensurate with core belief. Our behaviors are surest indicators of what we really believe. It is revealed in Jeremiah 6:14 that God is angered when our deepest wounds are treated only superficially—with band aids no less.

PERSONAL APPLICATION

8. When facing the fears and anxieties harbored in your deepest places, would you say that you *know* or that you *believe* Jesus as the Hero Redeemer?

HEARTBEAT OF THE STORY

15-20 MINUTES

Regarding redemption, God makes it clear that this part of the Larger Story is far too important to be left to chance. It's a job for Jesus and Jesus alone. This, however, does not mean that we are not invited to be a part of the Larger Story and the journey to redemption. We are both members of this story as well as being recipients of it.

ASK A VOLUNTEER TO READ THESE PASSAGES.

Everything in creation is being more or less held back. God reins it in until both creation and all the creatures are ready and can be released at the same moment into the glorious times ahead. Meanwhile, the joyful anticipation deepens.

ROMANS 8:20-21, THE MESSAGE

"I'll make up for the years of the locust, the great locust devastation—locusts savage, locusts deadly, fierce locusts, locusts of doom, that great locust invasion I sent your way.

JOEL 2:25, THE MESSAGE

OBSERVE

1. What do Romans 8:20-21 and Joel 2:25 reveal to you about the breadth and depth of redemption?

2. Describe the world as you might understand how it looks on the other side of God's ultimate and final restoration.

INTERPRET

My wife, Stasi, reads the end of novels first. Until recently, I never understood why. "I want to know how the story ends, to see if it's worth reading," she explained. "But doesn't knowing the end take away the drama?" I asked. "It only takes away the fear and frees you to enjoy the drama. Besides, some things are too important to be left to chance," she said, and turned back to her book.
*from John Eldredge's **The Sacred Romance.***

3. Do you believe, as Romans 8:20-21 says, that all is being held back? What does this mean for you personally?

[14]Now since the children have flesh and blood in common, He also shared in these, so that through His death He might destroy the one holding the power of death—that is, the Devil— [15]and free those who were held in slavery all their lives …

HEBREWS 2:14-15, HCSB

PERSONAL APPLICATION

4. What do you think the Hero Redeemer has been sent to redeem in your life? What has He come to free you from?

"Hero" is a Greek word meaning "he who protects and defends." Later, Latin speakers added a sense of "service" to the word. When we see the local police department's slogan, "to protect and serve," we could just as easily see the word "hero" in bold letters.

5. How do you think you could be more than what you have become?

PERSONAL EXPERIENCE

Although we will talk about it with great depth during our next meeting, the fact is that although Jesus was more than capable and even more than willing to heal physical maladies, that was not His central mission. His mission remains the same: bind up the broken hearts. Redemption is the central theme of the Larger Story.

Take a few minutes to put down on paper what you feel God revealing to you about what stands most in need of redemption in your life. It could be a work situation, a relational struggle either within your family or closest friends, or something from the past that has haunted you in one form or another for many years. The obstacles that stand between you and the person God has created you to be can only be thwarted by the Hero Redeemer of the Larger Story.

Once everyone has had an opportunity to write down some thoughts, close the group by praying for our Hero Redeemer to show His power in our stories.

Connecting with Your Story This Week

The take-home activity that follows is an individual experience. Plan to complete this exercise during a time you have allocated to being alone with God this week.

CONNECTING WITH MY STORY THIS WEEK

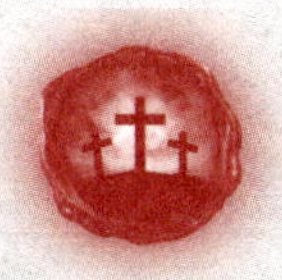

EXPERIENCE – IDENTIFYING THE VOWS

The following exercise is an intense experience included to help you identify the vows you have made that have resulted from the lies of the villain of the Larger Story. (See page 24-25 of Session 1.)

John 10:10 makes it very clear that the enemy seeks to steal, kill, and destroy. First Peter 5:8 adds to this that the villain of the Larger Story is constantly on the prowl, seeking what he may devour. One of the tactics of the enemy begins early in life with messages intended to kill our hearts, prevent us from trusting God, and drive us into isolation. These lies are most commonly associated with wounds in the deepest places. As we agree with some of these lies—not all of them—we make powerful vows, the "I'll never" statements. The child of divorce might vow never to be vulnerable to heartbreak. The victim of abuse might vow never to trust again. An individual shut off emotionally might vow to self-medicate in fantasy, addictions, or hyper-activity/busyness.

Scripture tells us to trust the Holy Spirit for how to pray. Without the help of the Holy Spirit, we will be unable to identify the wounds and the vows for what they are. Instead, we simply pass it off with quips like "It is what it is," "Well, I'm just a type A personality," or "I just don't go there." Self-medication in its various forms makes it difficult to know how to ask the Hero Redeemer to intercede on our behalf.

During a time totally devoted to listening to God this week, ask the Holy Spirit to reveal to you where you have agreed with the lies of the enemy. Prayerfully ask the Spirit of Truth to allow these vows to bubble up to the surface.

Be patient in this exercise. Although these revelations can come immediately, it is certainly not uncommon for responses to come over the course of days or even weeks.

SESSION FOUR

DANGEROUS ADVENTURES

AN EPIC ROMANCE

VILLAINS & MONSTERS TO BE SLAIN

A BEAUTY TO BE RESCUED

BETRAYAL & INTRIGUE

BATTLES TO BE FOUGHT AND WON

UNEXPECTED TWISTS & TURNS

GOOD ULTIMATELY TRIUMPHS OVER EVIL

A HERO-REDEEMER

PARADISE RESTORED

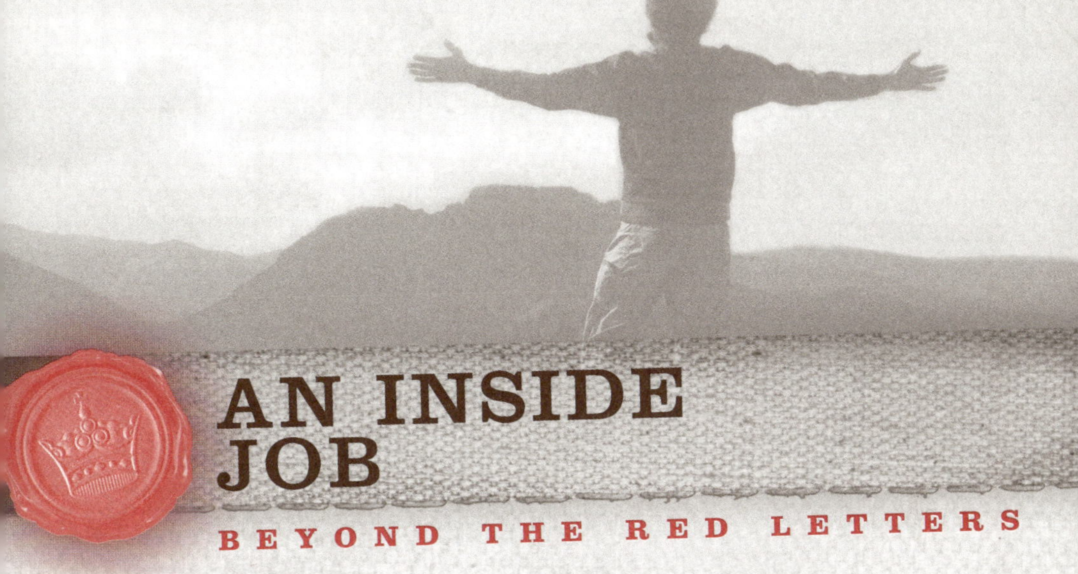

AN INSIDE JOB

BEYOND THE RED LETTERS

[8]For He had told him, "Come out of the man, you unclean spirit!"
[9]"What is your name?" He asked him. "My name is Legion," he
answered Him, "because we are many." [10]And he kept begging Him not
to send them out of the region.

MARK 5:8-10, HCSB

Then Jesus answered him, "What do you want Me to do for you?" "Rabbouni," the blind man told Him, "I want to see!"

MARK 10:51, HCSB

LARGER STORY SYNOPSIS

Held in the Larger Story is a beauty awaiting rescue. The process of being set free—being more than what you have become—is a lifelong event.

"Rescued from what?" you may ask. Even those of us that have no problem admitting that life is far from a bed of roses would be hard-pressed to align themselves with the damsel hidden away high in the castle tower or the man locked away in a dark and forlorn dungeon. But the Larger Story lens makes a distinction between the physical and the emotional and we see it over and over again in the Book of Mark. Clearly, as an all-knowing Jesus asks a blind Bartimaeus, "What do you want Me to do for you?" we must conclude that there is more. The business of rescuing the beauty in the Larger Story extends deep into the depths of the beauty's heart … this rescue is an inside job.

TIME TO DIALOG
- PUT PEOPLE AT EASE
- ENCOURAGE PARTICIPATION

OPENING SCENE

10-15 MINUTES

1. List adjectives that would normally describe a "beauty" requiring a rescue of some sort. What movies or other stories come to mind when you think about "a beauty to be rescued"?

2. How do people needing a rescue normally get into their predicament?

Talk about a time when you needed a rescue. Describe the situation and how you felt.

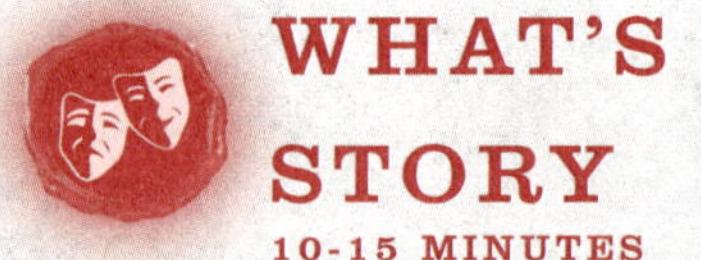

WHAT'S YOUR STORY

10-15 MINUTES

READ MARK 2:16-17 TO THE GROUP.

The religion scholars and Pharisees saw him keeping this kind of company and lit into his disciples: "What kind of example is this, acting cozy with the riff-raff?" Jesus, overhearing, shot back, "Who needs a doctor: the healthy or the sick? I'm here inviting the sin-sick, not the spiritually-fit."

MARK 2:16-17, THE MESSAGE

1. In Mark 2:16-17 Jesus makes a distinction between the sin-sick and the spiritually-fit. How do you think the spiritually-fit figure into His rescue mission? Did He also come for them? Why or why not?

2. What do you think is the difference between the two groups of people that Jesus describes in Mark 2:16-17?

Luke Skywalker: "I'm Luke Skywalker. I'm here to rescue you."
Princess Leia: "You're who?"
*from **Star Wars***

Last week's Connecting with My Story exercise included the prayerful examination of the vows that you may have made. While it's possible that you're among the spiritually-fit that Jesus describes, it's also possible that you're among the much larger group that Jesus has come to rescue. With this in mind, spend the rest of this portion of the session engaging the questions below.

3. Is it difficult to see yourself as a beauty to be rescued? If so, why do you think?

4. As you considered your own journey, at what places did you become aware of the enemy's attacks? Talk about the lies the enemy has deployed against you.

"BRING ME TO LIFE" PERFORMED BY EVANESCENCE
Words and Music by Amy Lee, Ben Moody, and David Hodges

(WAKE ME UP) WAKE ME UP INSIDE

(I CAN'T WAKE UP) WAKE ME UP INSIDE

(SAVE ME) CALL MY NAME AND SAVE ME FROM THE DARK

(WAKE ME UP) BID MY BLOOD TO RUN

(I CAN'T WAKE UP) BEFORE I COME UNDONE

(SAVE ME) SAVE ME FROM THE NOTHING I'VE BECOME

5. Share one vow that you have made. What events or circumstances do you think contributed most to your vulnerability in this area?

BEHIND THE SCENES

5-10 MINUTES

Let's take just a few minutes to flesh out the backstory at work as we pull the curtain back on the Larger Story.

➠ **ASK VOLUNTEERS TO READ THE FOLLOWING PASSAGES TO THE GROUP.**

> *1 After a few days, Jesus returned to Capernaum,*
> *and word got around that he was back home.*
> *2 A crowd gathered, jamming the entrance so*
> *no one could get in or out. He was teaching*
> *the Word. 3 They brought a paraplegic to him,*
> *carried by four men. 4 When they weren't able to*
> *get in because of the crowd, they removed part*
> *of the roof and lowered the paraplegic on his*
> *stretcher. 5 Impressed by their bold belief, Jesus*
> *said to the paraplegic, "Son, I forgive your sins."*
>
> ***MARK 2:1-5, THE MESSAGE***

All of that resolve. All of that work. All of that creativity. They cut through all the clutter to bring their friend to the fingertips of Jesus.

OBSERVE

1. According to Mark 2:1-5, what did Jesus do?

2. What do you think the man being carried felt at that moment?
   - ❒ Disappointment
   - ❒ Relief
   - ❒ Shame
   - ❒ Ecstasy
   - ❒ Joy
   - ❒ Depression
   - ❒ "See, I told you He wouldn't heal me!"
   - ❒ Anger
   - ❒ Other ________________

3. Why do you think the man felt that emotion?

4. If you were the paralytic described here, which emotion would you have felt?
   - ❒ Disappointment
   - ❒ Relief
   - ❒ Shame
   - ❒ Ecstasy
   - ❒ Joy
   - ❒ Depression
   - ❒ "See, I told you He wouldn't heal me!"
   - ❒ Anger
   - ❒ Other ________________

5. At that moment, what do you think the four friends felt?
   - ❐ Disappointment
   - ❐ Relief
   - ❐ Shame
   - ❐ Ecstasy
   - ❐ Joy
   - ❐ Depression
   - ❐ "See, I told you He wouldn't heal him!"
   - ❐ Anger
   - ❐ Other ________________

➡ **PERSONAL APPLICATION**

6. When you have needed healing, what have you sensed Jesus saying to you?

But this event does not end here.

➡ **ASK A VOLUNTEER TO READ MARK 2:6-8.**

> *[6]But some of the scribes were sitting there and reasoning in their hearts, [7]"Why does this man speak that way? He is blaspheming; who can forgive sins but God alone?" [8]Immediately Jesus, aware in His spirit that they were reasoning that way within themselves, said to them, "Why are you reasoning about these things in your hearts?*
>
> ***MARK 2:6-8, NASB***

Jesus turned the tables on His detractors. His question echoes today.

7. Which do you think was easier for Jesus—physical or spiritual healing?

[9]Which is simpler: to say to the paraplegic, 'I forgive your sins,' or say, 'Get up, take your stretcher, and start walking'? [10]Well, just so it's clear that I'm the Son of Man and authorized to do either, or both . . ." (he looked now at the paraplegic), [11]"Get up. Pick up your stretcher and go home." [12]And the man did it—got up, grabbed his stretcher, and walked out, with everyone there watching him. They rubbed their eyes, incredulous—and then praised God, saying, "We've never seen anything like this!"

MARK 2:9-12, THE MESSAGE

READ MARK 2:9-12 TO THE GROUP

Jesus often chose to heal in the physical world, or seen realm, as evidence of His mastery and power in the spiritual world, or unseen realm.

8. Read verse 10 above. What do you think Jesus is saying? Why do you think He chose to heal here?

UNFOLDING THE LARGER STORY

20-25 MINUTES

Stay Alive

The Villain of the Larger Story uses various schemes and tactics to hold us captive.

The thief comes only to steal and kill and destroy

JOHN 10:10, NASB

ASK VOLUNTEERS TO READ THIS PASSAGE.

1. We've already touched on some of the Villain's tactics. Take a few minutes to create a list of the schemes he uses to hold us captive.

[2]When He got out of the boat, immediately a man from the tombs with an unclean spirit met Him ... [3] And no one was able to bind him anymore, even with a chain ...

[5]Constantly, night and day, he was screaming among the tombs and in the mountains. ... [6]Seeing Jesus from a distance, he ran up and bowed down before Him; [7]and shouting with a loud voice, he said, "What business do we have with each other, Jesus, Son of the Most High God? I implore You by God, do not torment me!" [8]For He had been saying to him, "Come out of the man, you unclean spirit!" [9]And He was asking him, "What is your name?" And he said to Him, ***"My name is Legion; for we are many."*** *[10]And he began to implore Him earnestly not to send them out of the country.*

MARK 5:2-3,5-10, NASB (EMPHASIS ADDED)

OBSERVE

2. Why to you think Mark singled out the events identified in 5:2-3,5-10 as something to be recorded? What do you think makes this significant?

PERSONAL APPLICATION

3. What do you think verse 9 above reveals about the nature of the enemy and his obsession with taking us captive?

4. As the Larger Story unfolds and becomes clearer, how do you begin to understand your current condition and Jesus' rescue mission? What has been your deepest torment? What has kept you in chains?

Everything for a Reason

[47]When he heard that it was Jesus the
Nazarene, he began to cry out and say,
"Jesus, Son of David, have mercy on me!"
[48]Many were sternly telling him to be quiet,
but he kept crying out all the more, "Son
of David, have mercy on me!" [49]And Jesus
stopped and said, "Call him here." So they
called the blind man, saying to him, "Take
courage, stand up! He is calling for you."
[50]Throwing aside his cloak, he jumped up and
came to Jesus. [51]And answering him, Jesus
said, "What do you want Me to do for you?"
And the blind man said to Him, "Rabboni, I
want to regain my sight!"

MARK 10:47-51, NASB

INTERPRETATION

5. Do you think Jesus either didn't know or perhaps failed to notice Bartimaeus' particular malady—his blindness? If no, then why do you think he would have asked this question?

PERSONAL APPLICATION

6. What do you think Jesus' real question to Bartimaeus was? What do you think this question demanded of Bartimaeus and how do you think this question takes us deeper into the Larger Story and into the Hero's mission?

7. How would you answer Jesus' question: "What do you want Me to do for you?"

HEARTBEAT OF THE STORY

15-20 MINUTES

The Larger Story lens draws a line of demarcation between our secular journeys and our spiritual journeys. A troubled heart on the secular journey demands our attention. If it hurts we want it to get well. Our first option is to avoid pain and once that fails we medicate it in various ways. An untroubled heart on the secular journey is indicative of wellness and health.

1. How do you tend to medicate your pain?

2. Why do you think a person might self-medicate in place of allowing the Hero Redeemer to rescue him?

The spiritual journey, on the other hand, is absolutely sensitive to the loss of Eden. A troubled heart on the spiritual journey laments paradise lost and is able to remain in the pain. Remember WWJD? Jesus rejected shame and embraced pain.

3. If Jesus rejected shame and embraced pain, what do we tend to do? Why do you think so?

... keeping our eyes on Jesus, the source and perfecter of our faith, who for the joy that lay before Him endured a cross and despised the shame, and has sat down at the right hand of God's throne.
Hebrews 12:2

ASK A VOLUNTEER TO READ THE PASSAGE FROM JOHN 5.

*1 After this, a Jewish festival took place, and
Jesus went up to Jerusalem. 2 By the Sheep
Gate in Jerusalem there is a pool, called
Bethesda in Hebrew, which has five colonnades.
3 Within these lay a multitude of the sick—
blind, lame, and paralyzed [—waiting for the
moving of the water, because an angel would
go down into the pool from time to time and
stir up the water. Then the first one who got
in after the water was stirred up recovered
from whatever ailment he had]. 5 One man was
there who had been sick for 38 years. 6 When
Jesus saw him lying there and knew he had
already been there a long time, He said to him,
"Do you want to get well?" "7 Sir," the sick man
answered, "I don't have a man to put me into
the pool when the water is stirred up, but while
I'm coming, someone goes down ahead of me."
8 "Get up," Jesus told him, "pick up your bedroll
and walk!"*

JOHN 5:1-8, HCSB

4. How did Jesus "rescue" this man from his ailment?

OBSERVE

INTERPRET

5. John 5:1-8 describes a man that is literally paralyzed. In what ways do you think we can be emotionally paralyzed?

PERSONAL APPLICATION

6. Take a few minutes to discuss the ways you have been and, perhaps, continue to be emotionally paralyzed. Why do you think we often choose the secular journey over the spiritual journey?

Close in a time of directed prayer.

Connect with Your Story This Week

The take-home activities will greatly enhance your MORE experience. Be sure to allocate time this week to watch *Stranger Than Fiction* and engage the questions that follow.

CONNECTING WITH MY STORY THIS WEEK

STRANGER THAN FICTION

This week's Connecting with My Story gives you some options. Either by yourself, with a spouse or other close friend, or other members of the group, rent **Stranger Than Fiction** (2006, Will Ferrell, Maggie Gyllenhaal). Rent the movie, choose a night, and spend a little while enjoying the story. Let the host off the hook regarding food and volunteer to bring a fun finger food if you decide to make it a group activity.

1. What does Will Ferrell's character say he wants when asked by the corporate psychologist? How do you think this is in line with some of our previous discussions?

2. When we meet Harold Crick, would you say he is living in the Larger Story or the smaller stories? Give examples. What evidence is there that Harold is a "beauty" awaiting a rescue?

3. Talk about the various small stories as they relate to the Larger Story transpiring in **Stranger Than Fiction**.

4. How does what Harold Crick says he wants compare to what he actually gets as the story ends?

5. Discuss the implications resulting from the collision between Harold's life as it intersects the Larger Story that is being written.

SESSION FIVE

DANGEROUS ADVENTURES

AN EPIC ROMANCE

VILLAINS & MONSTERS TO BE SLAIN

A BEAUTY TO BE RESCUED

BETRAYAL & INTRIGUE

BATTLES TO BE FOUGHT AND WON

UNEXPECTED TWISTS & TURNS

GOOD ULTIMATELY TRIUMPHS OVER EVIL

A HERO-REDEEMER

PARADISE RESTORED

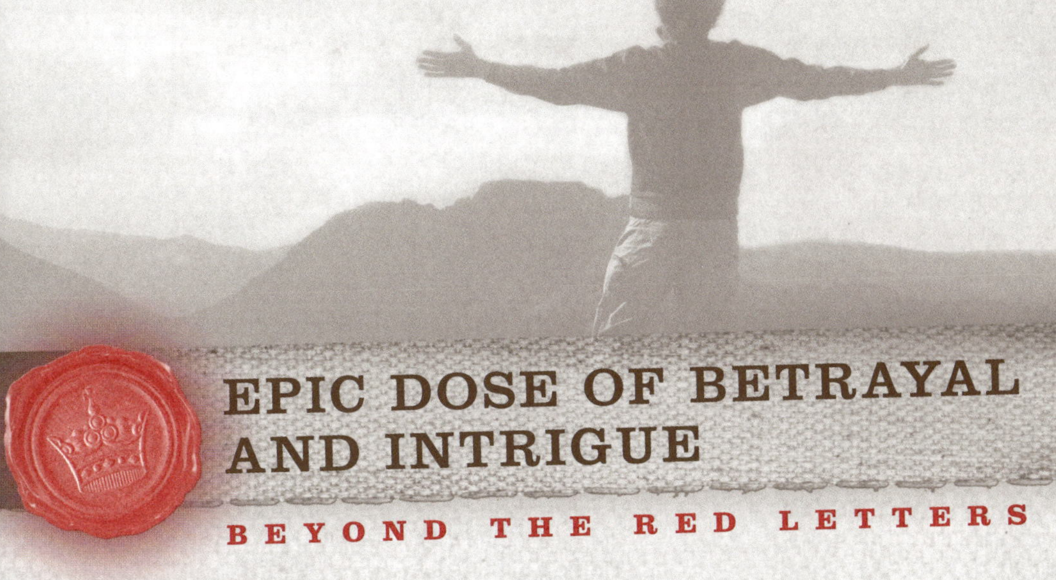

EPIC DOSE OF BETRAYAL AND INTRIGUE

BEYOND THE RED LETTERS

[10]Since He had healed many, all who had diseases were pressing toward Him to touch Him. [11]Whenever the unclean spirits saw Him, those possessed fell down before Him and cried out, "You are the Son of God!"

MARK 3:10-11, HCSB

[10]Then Judas Iscariot, one of the Twelve, went to the chief priests to hand Him over to them. [11]And when they heard this, they were glad and promised to give him silver. So he started looking for a good opportunity to betray Him.

MARK 14:10-11, HCSB

LARGER STORY SYNOPSIS

On the other side of the curtain lies a chess match between good and evil where betrayal and intrigue run wild.

Any epic story is earmarked by betrayal that leads to intrigue. The Larger Story revealed in the Book of Mark is full of secrets, mystery, the supernatural, and an overwhelming sense of magnitude, urgency, and significance. The drama begins almost immediately as the mere presence of Jesus disrupts some sort of natural understanding between and the unseen. "What do you want with us, Jesus of Nazareth? Have you come to destroy us?" the evil spirit asks. In the presence of Jesus, the forces of the unseen world are no longer indifferent; in the presence of Jesus the Larger Story is suddenly seen … supernatural intrigue and betrayal on the grandest of stages brought to the surface.

OPENING SCENE

10-15 MINUTES

Show clip from *Braveheart* (Chapter 14, see page 116 for instructions).

To open this meeting we're going to watch a scene from the epic film *Braveheart*.

1. Even without context of the story, how are you able to "feel" the weight of this moment?

2. What about Mel Gibson's character, William Wallace, suggests the magnitude of this betrayal?

Robert the Bruce: William Wallace fights for something that I never had. And I took it from him, when I betrayed him. I saw it in his face on the battlefield and it's tearing me apart.
Robert's Father: All men betray. All lose heart.
Robert the Bruce: I don't want to lose heart. I want to believe as he does.
*from **Braveheart***

3. Take a few minutes to talk about the other betrayals that have occurred when the stakes were high, either from fiction, history, or present day.

4. How does betrayal result in the intrigue of any story? How do you think it contributes to the drama?

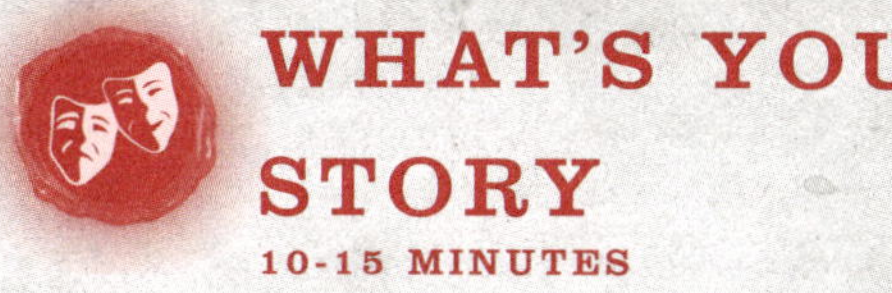

WHAT'S YOUR STORY

10-15 MINUTES

Take 2-3 minutes to describe the story and significant events of *Stranger Than Fiction*.

The Connecting With Your Story portion of "An Inside Job" involved watching *Stranger than Fiction*. During this What's Your Story experience we want to spend a few minutes talking about your story as it relates to what you encountered in the movie both as a way to reflect on the movie as well as establishing today's conversation.

1. By now you should be able to identify all the players in the Larger Story. Who are they? Can you identify their *Stranger Than Fiction* counterparts?

2. Did you find betrayal and intrigue in *Stranger Than Fiction*? If so, where?

This Life's dim Windows of the Soul Distort the Heavens from Pole to Pole. And lead you to Believe a Lie When you see with not thro the Eye.
from William Blake's ***The Everlasting Gospel***

BETWEEN THE LARGER STORY AND THE SMALLER STORIES IS WHERE THE UNSEEN AND SEEN WORLDS ARE MOST ENGAGED.

As Harold took a bite of Bavarian sugar cookie, he finally felt as if everything was going to be ok. Sometimes, when we lose ourselves in fear and despair, in routine and constancy, in hopelessness and tragedy, we can thank God for Bavarian sugar cookies.
*from **Stranger than Fiction***

The intrigue of the Larger Story reveals itself as it surfaces in our stories and collides with our own paths.

And He warned them to tell no one about Him.

MARK 8:30, NASB

3. Mark 8:30 suggests to us that Jesus had secrets. Where did you notice this aspect of intrigue show up in *Stranger than Fiction*? How does it make you feel to know that there are big chunks of information unavailable to you?

4. How does the Larger Story elbow its way into the life of Will Ferrell's character, Harold Crick? How have you sensed—either recently or in the past—the Larger Story elbowing its way into your own story?

5. In what ways have you experienced a situation during which your story collided with the Larger Story?

BEHIND THE SCENES

5-10 MINUTES

During Behind the Scenes we're going to take a look at some passages that speak into the betrayal and intrigue that's so intertwined with the Larger Story. This will lay a foundation for unfolding the Larger Story and provide the backstory for further conversation.

[12]Shining morning star, how you have fallen from the heavens! You destroyer of nations, you have been cut down to the ground. [13]You said to yourself: "I will ascend to the heavens; I will set up my throne above the stars of God.

ISAIAH 14:12-13, HCSB

ASK VOLUNTEERS TO READ THE VERSES BELOW.

[4]The serpent told the Woman, "You won't die. [5]God knows that the moment you eat from that tree, you'll see what's really going on. You'll be just like God, knowing everything, ranging all the way from good to evil."

GENESIS 3:4-5, THE MESSAGE

Cain said to his brother Abel, "Let's go out to the field." And while they were in the field, Cain attacked his brother Abel and killed him.

GENESIS 4:8, HCSB

So the LORD God asked the woman, "What is this you have done?"

GENESIS 3:13, HCSB

"One should rather die than be betrayed. There is no deceit in death. It delivers precisely what it has promised. Betrayal, though ... betrayal is the willful slaughter of hope."
Steven Dietz, playright

OBSERVATION

1. What do you think these verses reveal about the nature of betrayal, when it was introduced to the Larger Story, and how long it has been a part of both the physical and spiritual (seen and unseen) world?

INTERPRET

2. What do you think is revealed about the Villain's schemes in these verses?

ASK VOLUNTEERS TO READ THESE VERSES

And Elisha prayed, and said, "LORD, I pray, open his eyes that he may see." Then the LORD opened the eyes of the young man, and he saw. And behold, the mountain was full of horses and chariots of fire all around Elisha.

2 KINGS 6:17, NKJV

[4]On the twenty-fourth day of the first month, while I was by the bank of the great river, that is, the Tigris, [5]I lifted my eyes and looked, and behold, there was a certain man dressed in linen, whose waist was girded with a belt of pure gold of Uphaz. [6]His body also was like beryl, his face had the appearance of lightning, his eyes were like flaming torches, his arms and feet like the gleam of polished bronze, and the sound of his words like the sound of a tumult.

DANIEL 10:4-6, NASB

PERSONAL APPLICATION

3. Given the passages above, how are you affected by these glimpses into the intrigue of the Larger Story? Describe how you think it might feel to get a visual of the spiritually fantastic.

- Betrayal is the lowest form of relational destructiveness.
- Intrigue is mystery.

The intrigue often results from a betrayal of some kind. But whenever the Larger Story surfaces, you can be sure an element of intrigue will, too.

READ LUKE 4:28-30

[28]When they heard this, everyone in the synagogue was enraged.

[29]They got up, drove [Jesus] out of town, and brought Him to the edge of the hill their town was built on, intending to hurl Him over the cliff.

But He passed right through the crowd and went on His way.

LUKE 4:28-30, HCSB

4. There is obviously a mystical element in Luke 4:28-30. How do you think this would have looked in the seen world that we live in?

INTERPRET

5. How do you define "intrigue" as it relates to the Larger Story? Are you uncomfortable, excited, affirmed, or inspired by this element?

PERSONAL APPLICATION

6. Given that God is omniscient and all-powerful, why do you think He allows betrayal at the highest levels of reality? And why the intrigue? Don't you think it would be so much easier for appearance and reality to be the same?

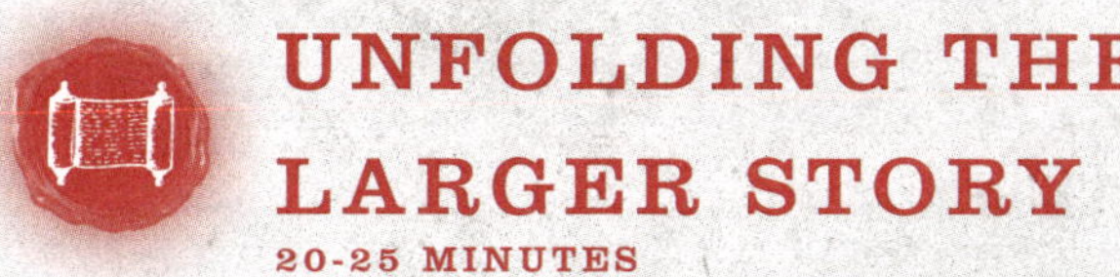

UNFOLDING THE LARGER STORY

20-25 MINUTES

Shhhhh

ASK VOLUNTEERS TO READ THE FOLLOWING VERSES.

And He would strongly warn them not to make Him known.

MARK 3:12, HCSB

Then He gave them strict orders that no one should know about this …

MARK 5:43, HCSB

Then He ordered them to tell no one …

MARK 7:36, HCSB

1. What do you think is going on in the passages above?

2. Given what you know about the Larger Story, why do you think Jesus would have secrets?

3. Do you think it's important that we get to the bottom of these secrets, figure it out? If so, how? If not, why not?

When Worlds Collide

ASK VOLUNTEERS TO READ THE FOLLOWING VERSES.

[23]Just then a man with an unclean spirit was in
their synagogue. He cried out, [24]"What do You
have to do with us, Jesus—Nazarene? Have You
come to destroy us? I know who You are—the
Holy One of God!" [25]But Jesus rebuked him and

said, "Be quiet, and come out of him!" [26]And the unclean spirit convulsed him, shouted with a loud voice, and came out of him. [27]Then they were all amazed, so they began to argue with one another, saying, "What is this? A new teaching with authority! He commands even the unclean spirits, and they obey Him." [28]His fame then spread throughout the entire vicinity of Galilee.

MARK 1:23-28, HCSB

4. In what ways does the intrigue of the Larger Story surface in the passage above?

5. What forces do you think cause the seen and unseen to appear on the same stage together in this sequence of events?

[10]Since He had healed many, all who had diseases were pressing toward Him to touch Him. [11]Whenever the unclean spirits saw Him, those possessed fell down before Him and cried out, "You are the Son of God!"

MARK 3:10-11, HCSB

6. According to Mark 3:10-11, what sort of people were "pressing toward" Jesus? What application do you think this has today?

OBSERVE

PERSONAL APPLICATION

7. What circumstances do you think would cause the seen and the unseen to share the stage in your own story?

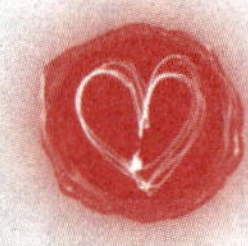

HEARTBEAT OF THE STORY

15-20 MINUTES

1. God invites you into the Larger Story while the enemy desperately wants to draw you into the smaller stories. How do you sense this aspect of reality at work in your own story?

2. How do you think you are betrayed by what you perceive? How do you think your heart may be able to detect the truth of the Larger Story?

3. Describe the smaller stories of your life. How do you think the enemy tries to draw you into the smaller stories?

4. Do the smaller stories have any intrigue at all? What is the difference between the intrigue in the Larger Story and the intrigue of the smaller stories?

5. When do you sense the intrigue of the Larger Story surrounding you most intensely?

Et tu, Brute?
Then fall, Caesar!
*from **Julius Caesar***

Connecting with Your Story this Week

Be sure to set aside time to engage the Reflection activity as you connect with your story.

CONNECTING WITH YOUR STORY

REFLECTION: QUESTIONS TO TAKE TO MY HEART AND TO GOD

The following question asks you to look into your heart and focus on your deepest feelings about yourself and God. Our behaviors are the best indicators of what we really believe. Use the space below each question to journal your thoughts as you sense the Holy Spirit's revelation.

QUESTIONS TO TAKE TO YOUR HEART

- Deuteronomy 29:29 says, "The hidden things belong to the Lord our God" (God's Word). How might I feel betrayed by someone close to me or even by God?

- What might be keeping me from a life of intrigue?

QUESTIONS TO TAKE TO GOD

- God, how do you feel about these feelings of betrayal?

- What intrigue could I be missing?

SESSION SIX

DANGEROUS ADVENTURES
AN EPIC ROMANCE
VILLAINS & MONSTERS TO BE SLAIN
A BEAUTY TO BE RESCUED
BETRAYAL & INTRIGUE
BATTLES TO BE FOUGHT AND WON
UNEXPECTED TWISTS & TURNS
GOOD ULTIMATELY TRIUMPHS OVER EVIL
A HERO-REDEEMER
PARADISE RESTORED

A WILD RIDE

BEYOND THE RED LETTERS

But in the next breath they were cutting him down: "He's just a carpenter—Mary's boy. We've known him since he was a kid. We know his brothers, James, Justus, Jude, and Simon, and his sisters. Who does he think he is?"

MARK 6:3, THE MESSAGE

[26]Though the king was deeply distressed, because of his oaths and the guests he did not want to refuse her. [27]The king immediately sent for an executioner and commanded him to bring John's head. So he went and beheaded him in prison,

MARK 6:26-27, HCSB

LARGER STORY SYNOPSIS

That the Larger Story is littered with unexpected twists and turns only serves to give meaning to our disorientation and confusion.

We want formulas. Or maybe we think we **need** formulas. Formulas are predictable and stable. They make sense and keep us oriented with our spiritual compasses. The simple facts, once taken collectively, suggest to us that the ride between the alpha and the omega—Act III of the Larger Story—can be a wild one. During these twists and turns we see God time and time again working alongside—fighting with us, intervening, redeeming us. The unexpected twists and turns reveal the dynamic nature of the Larger Story and call us into the wild.

OPTIONAL OPENING SCENE ON PAGE 118.

UNCERTAINTY, CONFUSION, PARADOX, AND DISORIENTATION ARE ALL PART OF THE JOURNEY THAT WE'RE ON.

OPENING SCENE

10-15 MINUTES

1. What do you do normally when you feel overwhelmed, disoriented, or confused?
   - ❐ Let it pass
   - ❐ Run away
   - ❐ Press into it
   - ❐ Ask for help
   - ❐ Medicate
   - ❐ Pray
   - ❐ Ignore it
   - ❐ Other __________

2. What twists and turns in your story have introduced the greatest degrees of disorientation?
   - ❐ New job
   - ❐ Falling in love
   - ❐ Death of __________
   - ❐ Loss of job
   - ❐ "I'm pregnant!"
   - ❐ Birth of child
   - ❐ Financial distress
   - ❐ Depression
   - ❐ 9/11
   - ❐ Tragedy
   - ❐ Other __________
   - ❐ Other __________

3. How do you think these plot turns compare to the unexpected twists we've come to expect from the Larger Story? How do you think your own plot twists are related to those of the Larger Story?

WHAT'S YOUR STORY

10-15 MINUTES

Break into groups of 2-4 people to talk about a time in your life when you experienced deep spiritual or emotional disorientation. Use the questions below as a guide.

1. What events led to this experience of disorientation? Describe some of the symptoms.

2. Describe the emotions associated with this period.

3. Briefly discuss the differences between your expectations and the reality you faced.

4. In what ways did these story-plot twists prompt you to wrestle with God?

Allow 8-10 minutes for group conversation before calling everyone back together. With the few minutes left ask if someone will tell a little bit of another's story.

"You always admire what you really don't understand."
Blaise Pascal, French mathematician and philosopher

BEHIND THE SCENES

5-10 MINUTES

ASK A VOLUNTEER TO READ ISAIAH 42:16

I will bring the blind by a way they did not know; I will lead them in paths they have not known ...

ISAIAH 42:16, NKJV

God is a mystery to be enjoyed, not a puzzle to be solved.

1. Why do you think God would choose a route through the unfamiliar as He guides us?

2. What do you think this says about His desire for us?

ASK A VOLUNTEER TO READ HEBREWS 11:35-37.

*35 Women received their dead raised to life again.
Some men were tortured, not accepting release,
so that they might gain a better resurrection,
36 and others experienced mockings and
scourgings, as well as bonds and imprisonment.
37 They were stoned, they were sawed in two,
they died by the sword, they wandered about
in sheepskins, in goatskins, destitute, afflicted,
and mistreated.*

HEBREWS 11:35-37, HCSB

The gospel will not be demystified. God will not be mocked by the pretensions of those who believe they might fully and certainly know His mind. Was that, after all, not the sin of the Garden?
*from Chuck Colson's **The Body***

3. Do you think the believers mentioned in Hebrews 11—known as the Hall of Faith—expected the sort of end described? What does this reveal about the severity of Larger Story twists and turns?

The hidden things belong to the Lord our God, but the revealed things belong to us and our children forever, so that we may follow all the words of this law.

DEUTERONOMY 29:29, HCSB

Summoning the crowd along with His disciples, He said to them, "If anyone wants to be My follower, he must deny himself, take up his cross, and follow Me.

MARK 8:34, HCSB

4. What do you think Deuteronomy 29:29 reveals about what you will know and what you will not know about the twists and turns of the Larger Story? What do you think Jesus meant when He told those on hand to deny themselves?

...My ways are higher than your ways, and My thoughts than your thoughts.
Isaiah 55:9

UNFOLDING THE LARGER STORY

20-25 MINUTES

What? Not What You Expected?

ASK VOLUNTEERS TO READ THE VERSES TO THE GROUP.

1 He went away from there and came to His hometown, and His disciples followed Him.
2 When the Sabbath came, He began to teach in the synagogue, and many who heard Him were astonished. "Where did this man get these things?" they said. "What is this wisdom given to Him, and how are these miracles performed by His hands?
3 Isn't this the carpenter, the son of Mary, and the brother of James, Joses, Judas, and Simon? And aren't His sisters here with us?" So they were offended by Him.

MARK 6:1-3, HCSB

INTERPRET

1. In what way is Mark 6:1-3 a twist of the Larger Story? What do you think the Villain expected the Messiah to be like?

2. Why do you think the people were "offended" by Jesus?

No Immunity

And He said, "Abba, Father! All things are possible for You. Take this cup away from Me. Nevertheless, not what I will, but what You will."

MARK 14:36, HCSB

"Now concerning that day or hour no one knows—neither the angels in heaven nor the Son—except the Father.

MARK 13:32, HCSB

OBSERVE

3. How do you think Jesus was affected by Larger Story twists and turns?

PERSONAL APPLICATION

4. What does the fact that even Jesus experienced disorientation say to you about the twists and turns of your own journey?

Mark 8:22-26 describes what scholars have referred to as the "imperfect miracle" because Jesus chose to put His hands on the blind man at Bethsaida twice. Clearly this was Jesus' choice given that other times all that He did was speak to heal while other times all He did was report that a person was already healed.

Look Closer

[22]Then they came to Bethsaida. They brought a blind man to Him and begged Him to touch him. [23]He took the blind man by the hand and brought him out of the village. Spitting on his eyes and laying His hands on him, He asked him, "Do you see anything?" [24]He looked up and said, "I see people—they look to me like trees walking." [25]Again Jesus placed His hands on the man's eyes, and he saw distinctly. He was cured and could see everything clearly.

MARK 8:22-25, HCSB

5. Why do you think Jesus would have chosen to put his hands on the blind man at Bethsaida twice? What do you think this says about the unexpected twists and turns of the Larger Story?

Not For the Faint of Heart

But Jesus let out a loud cry and breathed His last.

MARK 15:37, HCSB

"PEOPLE WISH TO BE SETTLED: ONLY AS FAR AS THEY ARE UNSETTLED IS THERE ANY HOPE FOR THEM."

RALPH WALDO EMERSON

6. How do you think Mark 15:37 flies in the face of formula and expectation?

7. Do you think the Villain saw this final twist coming? What effect does this final twist have on the Villain's scheme?

8. What implication does this ultimate twist have for you on the journey that you're currently on? How does this bring the Larger Story into greater focus for you?

HEARTBEAT OF THE STORY

15-20 MINUTES

1. In what ways do the unseen aspects of the Larger Story affect your bearing?

2. Think back to your time of disorientation that was brought to light earlier. Why do you think God allows you to experience these periods?

"I wanted a perfect ending. Now I've learned, the hard way, that some poems don't rhyme, and some stories don't have a clear beginning, middle, and end. Life is about not knowing, having to change, taking the moment and making the best of it, without knowing what's going to happen next. Delicious Ambiguity."
Gilda Radner 1946 – 1989, American comedienne

OUR GOD IS IN HEAVEN AND DOES WHATEVER HE PLEASES.
PSALM 115:3

3. Are there times when you do not sense God's presence? What do you think is the difference between silent and absent?

Gather the group into a circle, join hands, and close with prayer. Always pray as you feel led, but give everyone an opportunity to thank God for the adventure that He has called us into. Give members an opportunity to express how they feel when disoriented. Close in thankfulness knowing that God redeems it all.

4. How do you think God feels about it when you are experiencing pain and disorientation?

We've spent the last five sessions connecting what we're learning with our stories. We reflect on our experiences. Then we go through a new experience to see our lives through the lens of the Larger Story.

Connecting with your Story this Week

Again plan to allocate time this week to Connect with your story. During the coming week we'll take additional time to examine times of disorientation.

CONNECTING WITH YOUR STORY

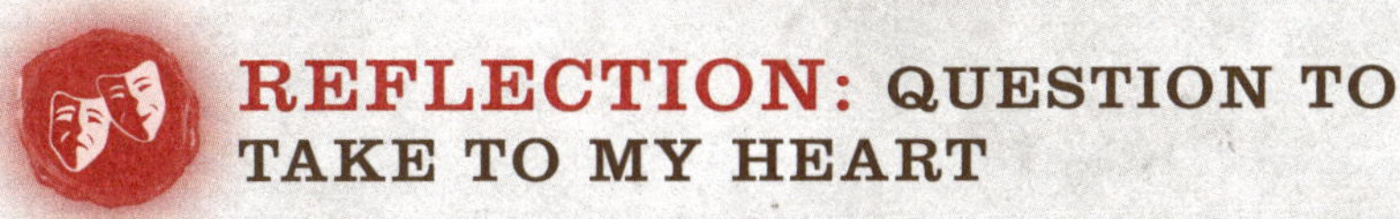

REFLECTION: QUESTION TO TAKE TO MY HEART

One of the best pictures of 1998 was **Saving Private Ryan**. Receiving several Academy Award nominations, **Saving Private Ryan** opens as Allied landing craft motor through the Normandy surf as the Allied invasion—know as D-Day—begins. When the doors open, US soldiers are greeted with terrifying machine gun fire. Machine gun fire killed some instantly. Disoriented, others drown. Those that made it to the beach found machine gun fire with even greater intensity. A sergeant heroically organizes a small group in an effort to make it to the wall—the first major step in breaking German lines. The noncoms have two choices: move forward or give in to the paralysis of fear. The officers are tasked to forge a collective effort of our chaos and the chaplains deliver last rights to the dying while medics take-the Herculean task of comforting the dying and aiding the wounded. In this scene, there is no mistaking the fact that the enemy is real, the stakes are high, and the ammo is live. In these moments, notions of reality are pointless.

The following questions ask you to reflect upon our study and this snapshot of history. Enter fully into disorientation as you answer these questions from your soul.

A QUESTION FOR YOUR HEART

With which soldiers do you most relate?

- Landing boat driver
- Officer
- Noncom
- Sergeant
- Medic
- Chaplain
- German machine gunner

- What do you think your answer tells you about how you view your role in the Larger Story?

SESSION SEVEN

DANGEROUS ADVENTURES
AN EPIC ROMANCE
VILLAINS & MONSTERS TO BE SLAIN
A BEAUTY TO BE RESCUED
BETRAYAL & INTRIGUE
BATTLES TO BE FOUGHT AND WON
UNEXPECTED TWISTS & TURNS
GOOD ULTIMATELY TRIUMPHS OVER EVIL
A HERO-REDEEMER
PARADISE RESTORED

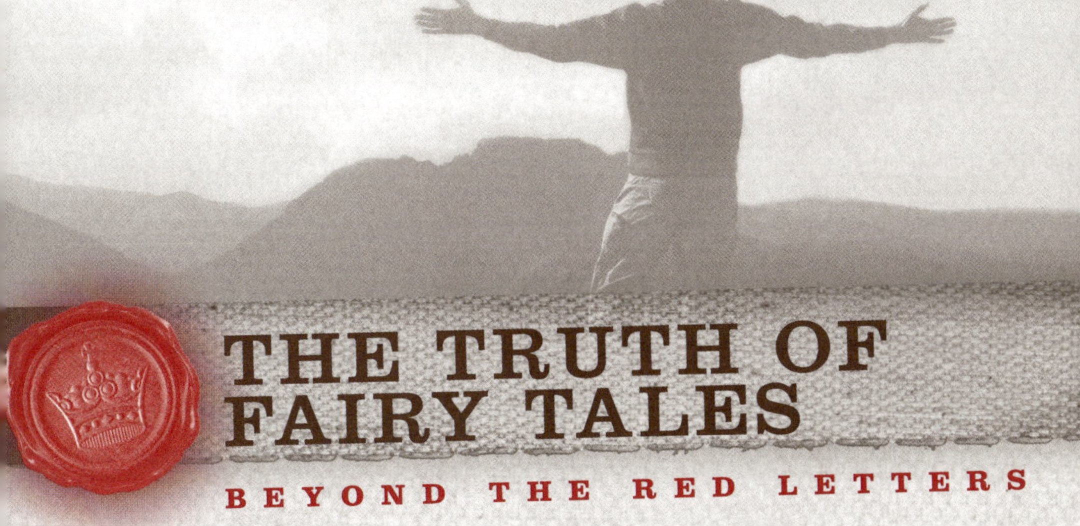

THE TRUTH OF FAIRY TALES

BEYOND THE RED LETTERS

He then began explaining things to them: "It is necessary that the Son of Man proceed to an ordeal of suffering, be tried and found guilty by the elders, high priests, and religion scholars, be killed, and after three days rise up alive."

MARK 8:31, THE MESSAGE

26 "Then they will see THE SON OF MAN COMING IN CLOUDS with great power and glory. 27 "And then He will send forth the angels, and will gather together His elect from the four winds, from the farthest end of the earth to the farthest end of heaven.

MARK 13:26-27, NASB

LARGER STORY SYNOPSIS

And just when the Villain believes the day is his, the scheme is foiled, evil is mocked, and good triumphs.

Despite overwhelming odds, Luke trusts the force and destroys the Death Star. Snow White gets her kiss, Cinderella's glass slipper fits, and Aurora is awakened by her prince. And so it is in the Larger Story as victory is snatched at the last minute from the Villain in an absolute and final conquest over death itself. Although battles remain and the enemy still holds sway, we know the Larger Story has found the ancient path that leads to restoration—the Eden that was lost comes again. Act IV of the Larger Story logs the ultimate triumph of good over evil ... but not yet.

- PUT PEOPLE AT EASE
- ENCOURAGE PARTICIPATION

List responses on a tear sheet, flip chart, or white board.

OPTIONAL OPENING SCENE ON PAGE 119.

OPENING SCENE

10-15 MINUTES

1. What are some of the fairy tales of our culture? List at least ten.

2. Add to the list what each of these has in common.

3. Think about how long some of these stories have been around. What characteristics and attributes do you think contribute to their staying power?

4. Do you believe in fairy tales? Why or why not?

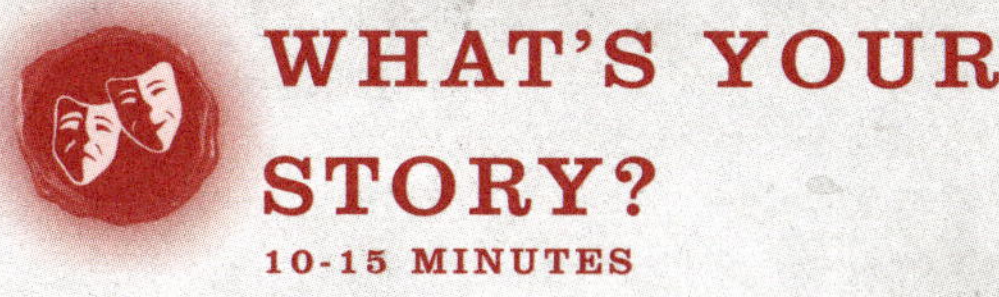

WHAT'S YOUR STORY?

10-15 MINUTES

As a part of the Connecting with My Story element of "A Wild Ride" you were asked to respond to a few questions that were directed toward your heart and to God. Take a few minutes to disclose how you felt the Holy Spirit was responding during this time.

ASK VOLUNTEERS TO DISCLOSE SOME OF WHAT THEY FELT DURING THIS EXERCISE.

1. What do your answers to the Connecting with My Story exercise reveal about disorientation in the Larger Story?

2. What do you think this might reveal about your core beliefs?

3. What are some of the events, circumstances, and experiences standing between us and the promises of Act IV? (See diagram on page 7.)

Act IV is our guarantee. Also guaranteed is redemption even though all things will be redeemed at various times and in varying degrees until all is absolutely redeemed and restored. In the meantime we must be mindful of the battle that is to be fought as participants of the Larger Story.

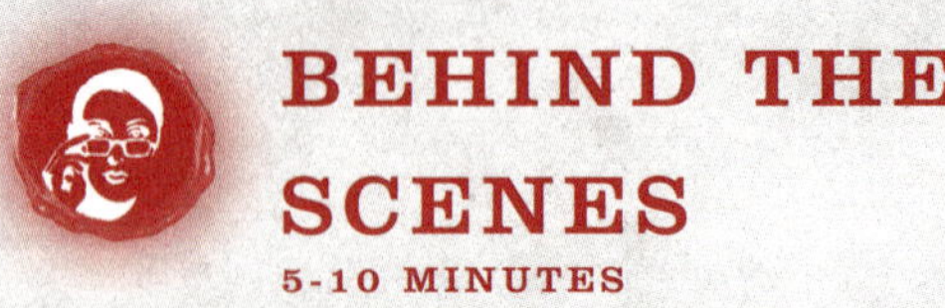

BEHIND THE SCENES

5-10 MINUTES

ASK A VOLUNTEER TO READ ISAIAH 9:18.

For wickedness burns like a fire that consumes thorns and briers and kindles the forest thickets so that they go up in a column of smoke.

ISAIAH 9:18, HCSB

INTERPRETATION

1. Talk briefly about some of the results of evil.

We have already discussed the Villain of the Larger Story, his schemes, and objectives. Introduced to us early in Genesis, the enemy remains busy in destruction. But we have also seen the agents of good not only standing against the great accuser, but also have scriptural accounts of how he is and will continue to be foiled.

ASK A VOLUNTEER TO READ THESE VERSES.

55 O Death, where is your victory? O Death, where is your sting? 56 Now the sting of death is sin, and the power of sin is the law. 57 But thanks be to God, who gives us the victory through our Lord Jesus Christ!

1 CORINTHIANS 15:55-57, HCSB

And I also say to you that you are Peter, and on this rock I will build My church, and the forces of Hades will not overpower it.

MATTHEW 16:18, HCSB

"God laughs with scorn at the obstinate folly of the arrogant. He ridicules with mockery. Contemptuous mockery may be evil's weapon against the glory of God, but it is also His weapon of destruction, which will eventually crush all who oppose Him."
Dan Allender

INTERPRETATION

2. What do 1 Corinthians 15:55-57 and Matthew 16:18 reveal about the ultimate power of good in the Larger Story?

"If you want a world where love is real, you must allow each person the freedom to choose."
from John Eldredge's ***Epic***

INTERPRETATION

3. Why do you think we must endure Act III of the Larger Story if the triumph of good is already set?

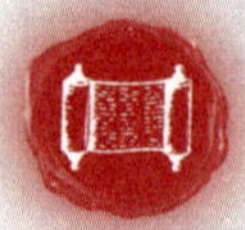

UNFOLDING THE LARGER STORY

20-25 MINUTES

Beneath the Surface

As we unfold this final aspect of the Larger Story from the Gospel of Mark, bear in mind that inherent in good triumphing over evil is a battle to be fought. The Larger Story is not a refuge from pain or danger.

ASK VOLUNTEERS TO READ THESE VERSES TO THE GROUP.

> *He looked them in the eye, one after another, angry now, furious at their hard-nosed religion.*
>
> ***MARK 3:5, THE MESSAGE***

OBSERVE

1. What sort of things do you think made Jesus angry?

APPLICATION

2. How do these things compare to the things that make you angry?

INTERPRET

3. Why do you think God allows anger?

ASK SEVERAL VOLUNTEERS TO READ THESE PASSAGES.

[1]Then He began to speak to them in parables: "A man planted a vineyard, put a fence around it, dug out a pit for a winepress, and built a watchtower. Then he leased it to tenant farmers and went away.

[2]At harvest time he sent a slave to the farmers to collect some of the fruit of the vineyard
from the farmers. [3]But they took him, beat
him, and sent him away empty-handed.
[4]Again he sent another slave to them, and
they hit him on the head and treated him shamefully.

MARK 12:1-4, HCSB

INTERPRET

4. How do you think God feels about evil? Why do you think He allows wickedness to endure?

Evil for Naught

[5]Then he sent another, and they killed that
one. He also sent many others; they beat some
and they killed some. [6]"He still had one to
send, a beloved son. Finally he sent him to
them, saying, 'They will respect my son.' [7]"But
those tenant farmers said among themselves, 'This is the heir. Come, let's kill him, and the inheritance will be ours!'

MARK 12:5-7, HCSB

[8]So they seized him, killed him, and threw him
out of the vineyard. [9]"Therefore, what will the
owner of the vineyard do? He will come and destroy the farmers and give the vineyard to others.

MARK 12:8-9, HCSB

OBSERVE

5. Mark 12 gives us Jesus' thoughts on where wickedness ultimately ends. What does Jesus say will happen?

6. Describe how the tables are turned on the tenant farmers. Do you think the tenant farmers thought they would get away with stealing the vineyard from the rightful heir? Why or why not? In what ways do you see this played out in the world around you?

HEARTBEAT OF THE STORY

10 – 15 MINUTES (OR MORE AS TIME ALLOWS)

1. Does evil seem to you to be too overwhelming at times? Maybe too present?

ASK A VOLUNTEER TO READ THESE VERSES.

[3]For although we are walking in the flesh, we do not wage war in a fleshly way,[4]since the weapons of our warfare are not fleshly, but are powerful through God for the demolition of strongholds.

We demolish arguments [5]and every high-minded thing that is raised up against the knowledge of God, taking every thought captive to the obedience of Christ.

2 CORINTHIANS 10:3-5, HCSB

2. Talk about one of the strongholds in your life. What fight do you think is uniquely yours?

3. In what ways has this conversation about the Larger Story as it is revealed in the Book of Mark helped you see these strongholds in a different light?

4. How has this helped you begin the process of demolishing these strongholds?

"The answer, in part, is to learn to mock evil. To mock like God, we must learn to violate evil by boasting in weakness and taunting death and suffering with the confident laughter of trust."
from ***The Cry of the Soul***

Indiana Jones: And what did you find, Dad?
Henry Jones: Me? Illumination.

Group Prayer: Be mindful of unique circumstances that have surfaced during this experience as you pray.

CLOSE BY CIRCLING UP FOR A PRAYER. BE SURE EVERYONE GETS A CHANCE TO THANK GOD FOR THE INVITATION INTO THE LARGER STORY, THEIR ROLES, AND THE HERO REDEEMER.

He also raised us up with Him and seated us with Him in the heavens, in Christ Jesus,
EPHESIANS 2:6, HCSB

5. What does Ephesians 2:6 say about your ability to address these strongholds, step aside, and allow good to triumph evil?

6. How do you think you can participate in the triumph of good in the Larger Story by mocking evil?

Connecting with My Story This Week

As a way to conclude this experience, spend the next several days—if not longer—in a listening prayer posture created to hear God speak to you. This time has been specifically created to allow God to reveal the name He has for you.

CONNECTING WITH MY STORY

The writer of the biography of Jesus we've been studying was named John and nicknamed Mark. The Bible is full of name-changing. A few notables include:
Abram to _______________ (Genesis 17:5)
Sarai to _______________ (Genesis 17:15)
Simon to _______________ (Matthew 16:16-19)
Saul to _______________ (Acts 13:9)

God has a special name for you as well. It's part of the ultimate victory in the story. Like a fighter pilot receives a call sign, God has a special name for those He loves.

> *"Anyone who has an ear should listen to what the Spirit says to the churches. I will give the victor some of the hidden manna. I will also give him a white stone, and on the stone a new name is inscribed that no one knows except the one who receives it.*
>
> ***REVELATION 2:17, HCSB***

- In an attitude of prayer, seek God during the next few days and ask Him what name He has for you.
- As you listen for God, you may hear many things. The enemy will use this as an opportunity to remind you of the arrows he has fired before.
- The name He has for you may touch the place where you are most wounded. Many who attempt this exercise dismiss their names because, "it couldn't be that."
- Once you think you know your new name, ask God to elaborate on why He chose it for you. Journal about what you hear and do your best to sort out the enemy's voice.
- The name is intended to be a special bond between God Almighty and you.
- Don't grow discouraged if you don't receive your name quickly. God wants to use this opportunity to grow you up. Don't resist.

NOTES

Other great small-group experiences from Serendipity House...

CANVAS

A DVD-driven small-group experience.

Emerging inside each of us is a unique work of art that reveals who we are and our vital role in the larger story. *Canvas* has been created to draw from deep within the stories God has given each of us, and to expose the beauty God is forging from the sum of our experiences. Using the power of story and art through DVD's and an Experience Guide for each group member, this small-group series brings a new multi-media dimension to Bible study. *Canvas* provides the context, the texture, and the materials for the journey. Through your story, your experiences, and the colors of your reality, God works to bring your role in the larger story to light.

VOLUME 1: DISTORTIONS

Distortions Kit 1574943367
Distortions Experience Guide . 1574943375

VOLUME 2: MYSTERY

Mystery Kit. 1574943561
Mystery Experience Guide . . . 157494357X

FOUNDATIONS

Experience the mystery for the first time. Again.

Jesus seemed to love paradox and often taught by asking questions rather than dumping information. It's an idea we can all connect with—an idea we all struggle with. At some point in our lives, we've had questions—"Who is God" and "Where was He when...". God can handle these questions and desires the intimacy that comes from working through them. *The Foundations of the Faith* series takes groups through this process.

Foundational Truths
1574943111

Knowing Jesus
1574943103

The Christian in a Postmodern World
1574941089

God and the Journey to Truth
1574941097

PICKING UP THE PIECES

Real help for real people living real life.

As our hearts engage in an epic battle, there are times we suffer deep, debilitating wounds. How do we make sense of these times and reconcile the reality of our pain with the goodness of God? Picking Up the Pieces is a series of honest, experiential Bible studies that will help you in the journey to recover your heart!

Redeeming the Tears. 1574941860
Stop the Madness. 1574941879
Recovering from Divorce 1574942220
Radical Reconciliation 1574942212
The Secret Seductress 1574942239
Surrendering the Secret 1574943502

REQUIRED SUPPLIES AND PREPARATION FOR EACH SESSION

DISCLAIMER: Serendipity by Lifeway does not approve of every word, action, or scene in the movies we've chosen to be a part of your MORE experience. Unfortunately, often the best stories include some pretty unsavory characters and behavior. Please note that these movies are not suitable for every situation. Please review each clip for suitability in your specific situation.

Session 1: The Stage is Set

Supplies: Poster or whiteboard and markers

Determine in advance which questions you want to engage. In order to build a foundation for understanding the Larger Story, this session is a little longer than the others. This may necessitate abridging the group experience in order to maximize the emotional energy. If you do decide to take this course be sure to encourage members to take the time to interact with the content on their own.

Opening Scene: Posterboard, white board, or tear sheets to display responses. You'll also need regular markers or dry erase markers.

What's Your Story: It's always a good idea to have pens and paper on hand for sub-groups.

Connecting with My Story: Be sure to articulate the options given here. In advance you may want to designate portions of Mark to read for this take-home activity.

OPTIONAL OPENING SCENE EXERCISE: PHOTO PHLASHBACK

Supplies:

- Poster board and marker
- Prize for winner of game (e.g., floating keychain, disposable camera, beach towel, flashlight, miniature car)
- Vacation pictures (brought by each member)
- Ballots numbered 1-10 with space to answer WHO? and WHERE?

Procedure for "Photo Phlashback"

- When you extend an invitation to attend your small group, ask each guest to bring a personal photograph from a vacation or trip. The older the picture, the better.
- When guests arrive, collect their pictures (in secret), have them fill out nametags, then point the way to the snacks and the other guests.

- Don't worry if some guests forget their photographs. Five or six photos are enough for a good game.
- Away from the eyes of the group, place the photographs on a poster board using a loop of transparent tape on the back of each picture.
- Number each photograph making sure to write on the poster board and not the picture.
- Gather the group together, hand out ballots, and present the posterboard.
- Each guest is to guess WHO is in each picture and WHERE the picture was taken (i.e., Disney World, Lake Lanier, Pacific Ocean, etc.).
- After everyone has voted, let each guest grade his or her own ballot. In numerical order, ask the photo's subject to reveal himself or herself, explain where the picture was taken, and share a short story about that trip.
- One point should be awarded for each correct answer. If you have 7 photographs, the highest possible point total is 14. In the case of a tie, let exactness break it. For example, if one ballot reads, "Branson, Mo." and the other reads, "Blue Velvet Theater, Branson", the one with more information wins.
- Present the prize to the winner
- Be sure to return the photos at the end of your small group session

1. How did you feel remembering the story behind your photograph? Check all that apply. Share your answers with the group if you like.
   - ❒ My mind was flooded with memories.
   - ❒ Bittersweet
   - ❒ Excited
   - ❒ Embarrassed
   - ❒ I'd forgotten some of that trip until just now.
   - ❒ Scared
   - ❒ Angry
   - ❒ I laugh when I see that picture.

2. Do you remember a place and time where you wish a photograph had been taken? Jot down a few words that describe the situation.
3. Dream a little. Where would you like to have your photograph made? With whom? List as many places and people as you like.

Session 2: Behind Enemy Lines

This experience has been created to explore with greater depth the adventure of a life with God. You'll want to be sure to help members identify the issues that might be preventative of such a life. The Larger

Story is not for the timid. Again, it's always helpful to review the session to find the Scriptures and questions you want to be sure to include in the conversation.

Be prepared to talk a little bit about the great adventure stories. These do not have to come from movies, but by using search engines you can find all kinds of instances that include *Into the Wild* (Krakauer) and *South with Endurance* (Shackleton). The obvious question surrounding this is, What makes these stories interesting?

OPTIONAL OPENING SCENE EXERCISE: I AM SPARTACUS

Supplies:

- Two hats or bowls
- Paper and pen
- List of heroes from below
- List of actions from below
- Scissors
- Lots of snacks and beverages

This optional activity is a way to have a few laughs and begin a conversation about dangerous missions and what it takes to get the job done.

Procedure for "I Am Spartacus"

1. Write the names of each hero or heroine from the list below on separate slips of paper.
2. Fold the slips and place them in a hat or bowl. Make sure you have more names than group members.
3. Make a list of everyday actions. (Provided are several examples.) Put these in a separate bowl.
4. Once all your group members have arrived and settled in, explain the rules of the game: "I'm going to pass two bowls around the group. The first bowl contains names of heroes and heroines from literature and the movies. The second bowl contains actions from everyday life. Please take one slip of paper from each bowl. You may look at the slips, but keep the information to yourself."
5. After everyone has selected two slips of paper, we're going to take turns acting out the strange combinations. Superman changing a diaper, for instance. This isn't charades. Use words, accents, props, and even makeshift costuming if you like.
6. The rest of the group will try to guess who you are and what you're doing.

7. Watch for those in your group for whom this is torture. Help the group be gentle with them, but encourage them to participate.
8. Have a camera handy for photographs. Capture these memories for your group.

Heroes and Heroines

- Superman
- Wonder Woman
- Elastigirl (Mrs. Incredible)
- Spiderman/Peter Parker
- Cinderella
- Indiana Jones
- Rocky Balboa
- Dorothy Gale (Wizard of Oz)
- Tarzan
- Eowyn (Lord of the Rings)
- Hermione Granger (Harry Potter)
- Lucy Pevensie (Chronicles of Narnia)
- T-800 (The Terminator)

Everyday Actions

- Starting a temperamental lawnmower
- Changing a diaper
- Fighting bumper-to-bumper traffic
- Running in a road race
- Receptionist answering multiple lines in a busy office
- Fighting with a computer
- Cooking a romantic meal
- Trying to stay awake during a boring meeting

Session 3: A Force of Nature

(READ DISCLAIMER ON PAGE 110)
The Hero-Redeemer is central to the action of the Larger Story. A good companion piece to this session is Larry Crabb's *Shattered Dreams* which examines the Book of Ruth. Be sure members are able to distinguish the Hero Redeemer of the Larger Story from the other heroes around us. While there are great women and men in our world, there is only one Christ and He has called us into His story.

Need:
TV/DVD player
DVD: *Gladiator* (Russell Crowe, 2000)
Cue the movie to chapter 16: My Name is Gladiator

Opening Scene:

- Play the DVD from the cue to the 4:00 mark
- Once the scene ends, hit the power button on the television. Then stop the DVD and turn the DVD player off.

Connecting with My Story This Week
Take a moment to direct the group's attention to this. This is predicated on the belief that while God works to form us spiritually, the enemy works to de-form us. The enemy discovers our wounds and speaks lies into thsm. Over time we agree and, as a result, we make vows. These vows take us farther away from the men and women we have been created to be. Like the starry Mufasa tells Simba in *The Lion King*, "You are more than what you have become." This part of the journey is crucial to the MORE series.

Session 4: An Inside Job

(READ DISCLAIMER ON PAGE 110)
Spend some time setting up the notion that the beauty to be rescued is ... you. Healing continues even in the life of a believer—even in a newly converted heart. The fact is, many people—especially men—can show an unwillingness to engage in this conversation. First, we're not taught to express what many consider to be weakness. Also, while women have had to adopt and become comfortable with so many metaphors with a masculine bent, men have not been asked to relate metaphorically to comparisons more feminine in nature. The experience will be much better if you take a few minutes to address these ideas so members can understand what they're feeling.

Remind members that *Stranger Than Fiction* will be a centerpiece for your next MORE experience. So it's doubly beneficial to set aside time to watch the movie and participate in Connecting with My Story.

Session 5: An Epic Dose of Betrayal and Intrigue

(READ DISCLAIMER ON PAGE 110)
Need:

- TV/DVD player
- DVD: *Braveheart* (Mel Gibson, 1995)
- Cue the movie to chapter 14: Unity and Betrayal

Opening Scene:
Begin the movie clip as William Wallace enters the council meeting (about 1:55) and continue through to the betrayal scene toward the conclusion of the battle sequence. At first it looks as if Wallace and the Scots may come out on top, but the mood quickly sours when it becomes evident the deck is stacked against him. Be sure that members pay attention to Gibson's body language when his horsebacked pursuit ends with the realization that Robert the Bruce has sold him out.

Only 10-15 minutes is allocated to Opening Scene and the clip itself borders on 12 minutes. Try to keep interaction at a quick pace while giving everyone an opportunity to speak. Refer back to this scene throughout the experience.

Once the scene ends, hit the power button on the television. Then stop the DVD and turn the DVD player off.

Session 6: A Wild Ride

Supplies:

- Paper and pens/pencils

It's a good idea to do your own research on Mark 8:22-25. Consult various commentaries or leaders. The Internet is always a good source as well.

This experience could just as easily be called "Disorientation." Although "twists and turns" in a movie usually translates into great entertainment, most often the same in life is anything but fun. Disorientation is very serious, and there shouldn't be anyone in the group that cannot relate either at a personal level or that has walked with someone else through unexpected adversity. Throughout this portion you'll be addressing these times as they relate to the Larger Story. The MORE position is that Twists and Turns could very easily be a sub-point of Dangerous Adventure, but because formulas are so common and the formula not working is just as common, it needs to be treated as a separate element of the Larger Story. Be very prayerful as you head into "A Wild Ride."

What's Your Story
It's always a good idea to have pens/pencils on hand for sub-group activity.

OPTIONAL OPENING SCENE EXERCISE: POP! GOES THE KERNEL

"Pop! Goes the Kernel" is a demonstration of the "not knowing when" phenomenon. As members wait ask them to pay attention to how they feel. Describe feelings of anticipation, expectancy, fear of the unknown.

Supplies:

- One inexpensive metal spoon per group member
- Non-microwave popcorn
- Cooking oil (or cooking spray)
- Eye dropper (optional)
- Matches or lighter
- One tea light candle per group member
- Small prize for the winner
- Snacks and beverages (perhaps with a popcorn theme)

Procedure for Setting the Stage: "Pop! Goes the Kernel"

- Space out the tea light candles along a kitchen counter or around a kitchen island
- Invite your group members to pick a tea light
- Hand out the spoons
- Pass around the oil and eye dropper or cooking spray. Every member needs to add just a little oil to the inside part of the spoon.
- Each member gets three kernels of popcorn
- Light the tea lights
- Put the spoons in the flame (Note: Some carbon might build up on the bottom, but should come off in washing.)
- As the group leader, you are the judge. Watch for all three kernels to pop. This should take about two minutes. (The pops will not be very big because the heat is not as high as other popcorn cooking environments.)

In some form or fashion, express these thoughts during this exercise and follow-up discussion:
A popcorn kernel is a good metaphor for the tension we feel in our lives. We each long for a metamorphosis. We wait. We endure heat. We can't predict when it will happen. We hope and pray. Despite our best efforts to the contrary, we look around at others to see how their lives are progressing.

1. What would have made the popcorn kernels pop faster?
2. Talk about how you felt during this exercise.

Session 7: The Truth in Fairy Tales

Tonight's conversation includes the classic "good vs. evil." Since everyone should be familiar with this paradigm, be sure to draw everyone into the group discussion early in order to get the most out of your time. We'll be drawing particular attention to the promise that good will ultimately triumph, but battles remain.

Since this is the last session, if food and beverage isn't a normal part of your group life, make tonight special and festive by asking members to bring snacks and finger foods. If food is typical of your group, consider going beyond the norm for this last conversation.

Opening Scene:
Think in advance about some of the fairy tales and adventure stories familiar to our culture. Here are a few to get you started:
"The Ugly Duckling"
Sleeping Beauty
Snow White
Rumplestiltsken
The Lord of the Rings
"Little Red Riding Hood"
Cinderella
The Odyssey
The Wizard of Oz

Connecting with My Story:
All of these exercises are important, but this week's maybe even more so given its intimate nature and its open-endedness. It's a good idea to provide additional explanation and give special attention to this part of *Beyond the Red Letters*.

OPTIONAL OPENING SCENE EXERCISE: PRINCE OF THIEVES

(READ DISCLAIMER ON PAGE 110)
Procedure for Movie Excerpt from Robin Hood: Prince of Thieves.

- Set the TV to a comfortable volume.
- Cue up the DVD to chapter 11, "Will's Bargain" (0:42:17 on the timer, side 2 of double-sided disc. The city prepares for the wedding while Hood's men prepare for an ambush. A little boy sees Will Scarlett's sword right before the heralds' trumpets blow).
- Press pause
- Turn the TV off
- When you reach the cue during the group session, press play on

the DVD remote and then turn the TV on. (Note: Not all remotes work the same way. Experiment with your remote for a smooth beginning to this clip.)

- Play until the credits begin to roll (1:03:53).
- Lead the emotion. Without exaggerating, gasp, cheer, applaud, etc. Use your own reactions to help your group include theirs.
- Turn off the TV
- Press stop on the DVD

The legend of Robin Hood is one of the oldest examples of the Larger Story in literature. All of the players make their appearance. The cardinal is a pawn of an evil prince and his local magistrate, the Sheriff of Nottingham. The sheriff has captured Marian and intends to force her to marry him. The marriage will cement political gains for the future and grant more power. Meanwhile, the sheriff's minions have gathered up several criminals—including some of Robin of Loxley's men—for hanging. The entire kingdom shows up for the executions and wedding. This show of force will bring Robin to his knees. The wedding, planned for a few hours later, will be a triumph for evil.

Leader: Play the movie clip according to the directions.

1. As you watch this clip, count the obstacles Robin and his band face during their rescue attempt.
   Obstacles: ______________________

2. Count the main enemies encountered as well. What types of enemies show up on the scene? What happens to the enemies?

3. A sword plays a significant role. What does the sword represent in the Larger Story? What might a sword represent in your life?

WELCOME TO COMMUNITY!

Meeting together to study God's Word and experience life together is an exciting adventure. A small group is ... *a group of people unwilling to settle for anything less than redemptive community.*

Core Values

Community: God is relational, so He created us to live in relationship with Him and each other. Authentic community involves sharing life together and connecting on many levels with others in our group.

Group Process: Developing authentic community takes time. It's a journey of sharing our stories with each other and learning together. Every healthy group goes through stages over a period of months or years. We begin with the birth of a new group, deepen our relationships in the growth and development stages, and ultimately multiply to form other new groups.

Interactive Bible Study: God gave the Bible as our instruction manual for life. We need to deepen our understanding of God's Word. People learn and remember more as they wrestle with truth and learn from others. Bible discovery and group interaction enhance growth.

Experiential Growth: Beyond solely reading, studying, and dissecting the Bible, being a disciple of Christ involves reunifying knowledge with experience. We do this by taking questions to God, opening a dialog with our hearts (instead of killing desire), and utilizing other ways to listen to God speak (other people, nature, art, movies, circumstances). Experiential growth is always grounded in the Bible as God's primary revelation and our ultimate truth-source.

Power of God: Processes and strategies will be ineffective unless we invite and embrace the presence and power of God. In order to experience community and growth, Jesus needs to be the centerpiece of our group experiences and the Holy Spirit must be at work.

Redemptive Community: Healing best occurs within the context of community and relationships. It's vital to see ourselves through the eyes of others, share our stories, and ultimately find freedom from the secrets and lies that enslave our souls.

Mission: God has invited us into a larger story with a great mission of setting captives free and healing the broken-hearted (Isaiah 61:1-2). However, we can only join in this mission to the degree that we've let Jesus bind up our wounds and set us free. Others will be attracted to an authentic redemptive community.

SHARING YOUR STORIES

The sessions of *Beyond the Red Letters* are designed to help you share a little of your personal lives with the other people in your group as you experience MORE. Through your time together, each member of the group is encouraged to move from low risk, less personal sharing to higher risk communication. Real community will not develop apart from increasing intimacy of the group over time.

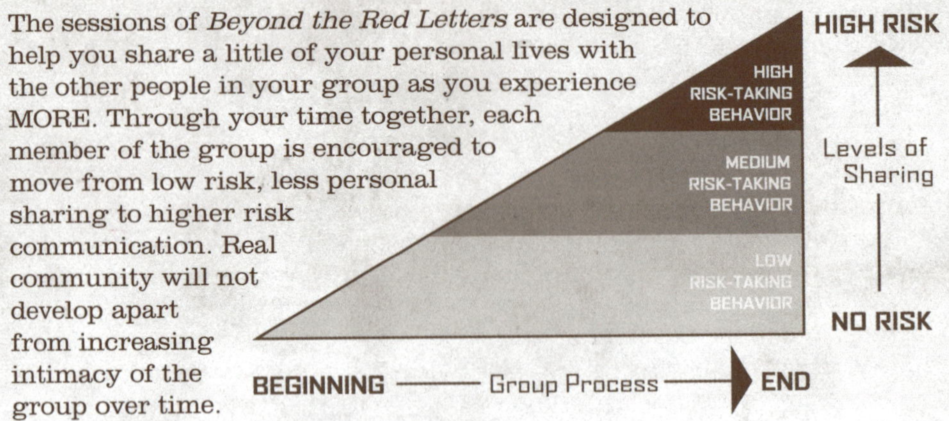

SHARING YOUR LIVES

As you share your lives together during this time, it is important to recognize that it is God who has brought each person to this group, gifting the individuals to play a vital role in the group (1 Corinthians 12:1). Each of you was uniquely designed to contribute in your own unique way to building into the lives of the other people in your group. As you get to know one another better, consider the following four areas that will be unique for each person. These areas will help you get a "grip" on how you can better support others and how they can support you.

G – Spiritual Gifts: God has given you unique spiritual gifts (1 Corinthians 12; Romans 12:3-8; Ephesians 4:1-16; etc.).

R – Resources: You have resources that perhaps only you can share, including skill, abilities, possessions, money, and time (Acts 2:44-47; Ecclesiastes 4:9-12, etc.).

I – Individual Experiences: You have past experiences, both good and bad, that God can use to strengthen others (2 Corinthians 1:3-7; Romans 8:28, etc.).

P – Passions: There are things that excite and motivate you. God has given you those desires and passions to use for His purposes (Psalm 37:4,23; Proverbs 3:5-6,13-18; etc.).

To better understand how a group should function and develop in these four areas, consider going through the Serendipity study entitled *Great Beginnings.*

GROUP COVENANT

As you begin this study, it is important that your group covenant together, agreeing to live out important group values. Once these values are agreed upon, your group will be on its way to experiencing true Christian community. It's very important that your group discuss these values—preferably as you begin this study. The first session would be most appropriate.

* ***Priority:*** While we are in this group, we will give the group meetings priority.

* ***Participation:*** Everyone is encouraged to participate and no one dominates.

* ***Respect:*** Everyone is given the right to his or her own opinions, and all questions are encouraged and respected.

* ***Confidentiality:*** Anything that is said in our meetings is never repeated outside the meeting without permission.

* ***Life Change:*** We will regularly assess our progress toward applying the "steps" to an amazing marriage. We will complete the "Taking it Home" activities to reinforce what we are learning and better integrate those lessons into our lives.

* ***Care and Support:*** Permission is given to call upon each other at any time, especially in times of crisis. The group will provide care for every member.

* ***Accountability:*** We agree to let the members of our group hold us accountable to commitments we make in whatever loving ways we decide upon. Unsolicited advice giving is not permitted.

* ***Empty Chair:*** Our group will work together to fill the empty chair with an unchurched person or couple.

* ***Mission:*** We agree as a group to reach out and invite others to join us and to work toward multiplication of our group to form new groups.

* ***Ministry:*** We will encourage one another to volunteer to serve in a ministry and to support missions work by giving financially and/or personally serving.

I agree to all of the above____________________________ date: ________

LEADING A SMALL GROUP

You will find a great deal of helpful information in this section that will be crucial for success as you lead your group.

Reading through this and utilizing the suggested principles and practices will greatly enhance the group experience. You need to accept the limitations of leadership. You cannot transform a life. You must lead your group to the Bible, the Holy Spirit, and the power of Christian community. By doing so your group will have all the tools necessary to draw closer to God and each other, and to experiencing heart transformation.

Make the following things available at each session:

- *Beyond the Red Letters* book for each attendee
- Bible for each attendee
- Snacks and refreshments
- Pens or pencils for each attendee

The Setting and General Tips:

1. Prepare for each meeting by reviewing the material, praying for each group member, asking the Holy Spirit to join you, and making Jesus the centerpiece of every experience.

2. Create the right environment by making sure chairs are arranged so each person can see the eyes of every other attendee. Set the room temperature at 69 degrees. If meeting in a home, make sure pets are in a location where they cannot interrupt the meeting. Request that cell phones are turned off unless someone is expecting an emergency call. Have music playing as people arrive (volume low enough for people to converse) and, if possible, burn a sweet-smelling candle.

3. Try to have soft drinks and coffee available for early arrivals.

4. Have someone with the spiritual gift of hospitality ready to make any new attendees feel welcome.

5. Be sure there is adequate lighting so that everyone can read without straining.

6. Connect with group members away from group time. The amount of participation you have during your group meetings is directly related to the amount of time you connect with your group members away from the meeting time.

7. There are four types of questions used in each session: Observation (What is the passage telling us?), Interpretation (What does the passage mean?), Self-revelation (How am I doing in light of the truth unveiled?), and Application (Now that I know what I know, what will I do to integrate this truth into my life?). You won't be able to use all the questions in each study, but be sure to use some from each.

8. Don't get impatient about the depth of relationship group members are experiencing. Building real Christian Community takes time.

9. Be sure pens and/or pencils are available for attendees at each meeting.

10. Never ask someone to pray aloud without first getting their permission.

Leading Meetings:

1. Before the icebreakers, do not say, "Now we're going to do an icebreaker." The meeting should feel like a conversation from beginning to end, not a classroom experience.

2. Be certain every member responds to the icebreaker questions. The goal is for every person to hear his or her own voice early in the meeting. People will then feel comfortable to converse later on. If members can't think of a response, let them know you'll come back to them after the others have spoken.

3. Remember, a great group leader talks less than 10% of the time. If you ask a question and no one answers, just wait. If you create an environment where you fill the gaps of silence, the group will quickly learn they needn't join you in the conversation.

4. Don't be hesitant to call people by name as you ask them to respond to questions or to give their opinions. Be sensitive, but engage everyone in the conversation.

5. Don't ask people to read aloud unless you have gotten their permission prior to the meeting. Feel free to ask for volunteers to read.

6. Watch your time. If discussion time is extending past the time limits suggested, offer to the option of pressing on into other discussions or continuing the current session into your next meeting. REMEMBER: People and their needs are always more important than completing all the questions.

GROUP DIRECTORY

Write your name on this page. Pass your books around and ask your group members to fill in their names and contact information in each other's books.

Your Name: ______________________________

Name: ______________________
Address: ______________________
City: ______________________
Zip Code: ______________________
Home Phone: ______________________
Mobile Phone: ______________________
E-mail: ______________________

Name: ______________________
Address: ______________________
City: ______________________
Zip Code: ______________________
Home Phone: ______________________
Mobile Phone: ______________________
E-mail: ______________________

Name: ______________________
Address: ______________________
City: ______________________
Zip Code: ______________________
Home Phone: ______________________
Mobile Phone: ______________________
E-mail: ______________________

Name: ______________________
Address: ______________________
City: ______________________
Zip Code: ______________________
Home Phone: ______________________
Mobile Phone: ______________________
E-mail: ______________________

Name: ______________________
Address: ______________________
City: ______________________
Zip Code: ______________________
Home Phone: ______________________
Mobile Phone: ______________________
E-mail: ______________________

Name: ______________________
Address: ______________________
City: ______________________
Zip Code: ______________________
Home Phone: ______________________
Mobile Phone: ______________________
E-mail: ______________________

Name: ______________________
Address: ______________________
City: ______________________
Zip Code: ______________________
Home Phone: ______________________
Mobile Phone: ______________________
E-mail: ______________________

Name: ______________________
Address: ______________________
City: ______________________
Zip Code: ______________________
Home Phone: ______________________
Mobile Phone: ______________________
E-mail: ______________________

Name: ______________________
Address: ______________________
City: ______________________
Zip Code: ______________________
Home Phone: ______________________
Mobile Phone: ______________________
E-mail: ______________________

Name: ______________________
Address: ______________________
City: ______________________
Zip Code: ______________________
Home Phone: ______________________
Mobile Phone: ______________________
E-mail: ______________________

Name: ______________________
Address: ______________________
City: ______________________
Zip Code: ______________________
Home Phone: ______________________
Mobile Phone: ______________________
E-mail: ______________________

Name: ______________________
Address: ______________________
City: ______________________
Zip Code: ______________________
Home Phone: ______________________
Mobile Phone: ______________________
E-mail: ______________________

NOTES

ACKNOWLEDGMENTS:

MORE. Series Creator and Author – Ron Keck

Ron currently serves as publisher at Serendipity House as well as Managing Director of LifeWay Christian Resources. He is a graduate of Dallas Theological Seminary. He and his wife, Brenda, reside in Thompson Station, TN. Ron has written two studies in our God and the Arts series as well as *Song of Songs: The Epic Romance*.

We would be very much remiss if we did not acknowledge the content of *Epic: The Story God Is Telling and the Role that Is Yours to Play* by John Eldredge. John's significant contributions to our understanding of the Larger Story has paved the way for experiences such as *Beyond the Red Letters* and other MORE experiences.

Co-writer and Editor: Brian Daniel
Cover and Interior Design: Scott Lee Designs
Research and Support: Mark Whitlock
Copyeditor: Justine Scheriger

We hope for captives to be set free, broken hearts to be binded up and restored, sight for the blind, and the ashes of the story replaced by beauty (Isaiah 61:1-3).